Coloring Book

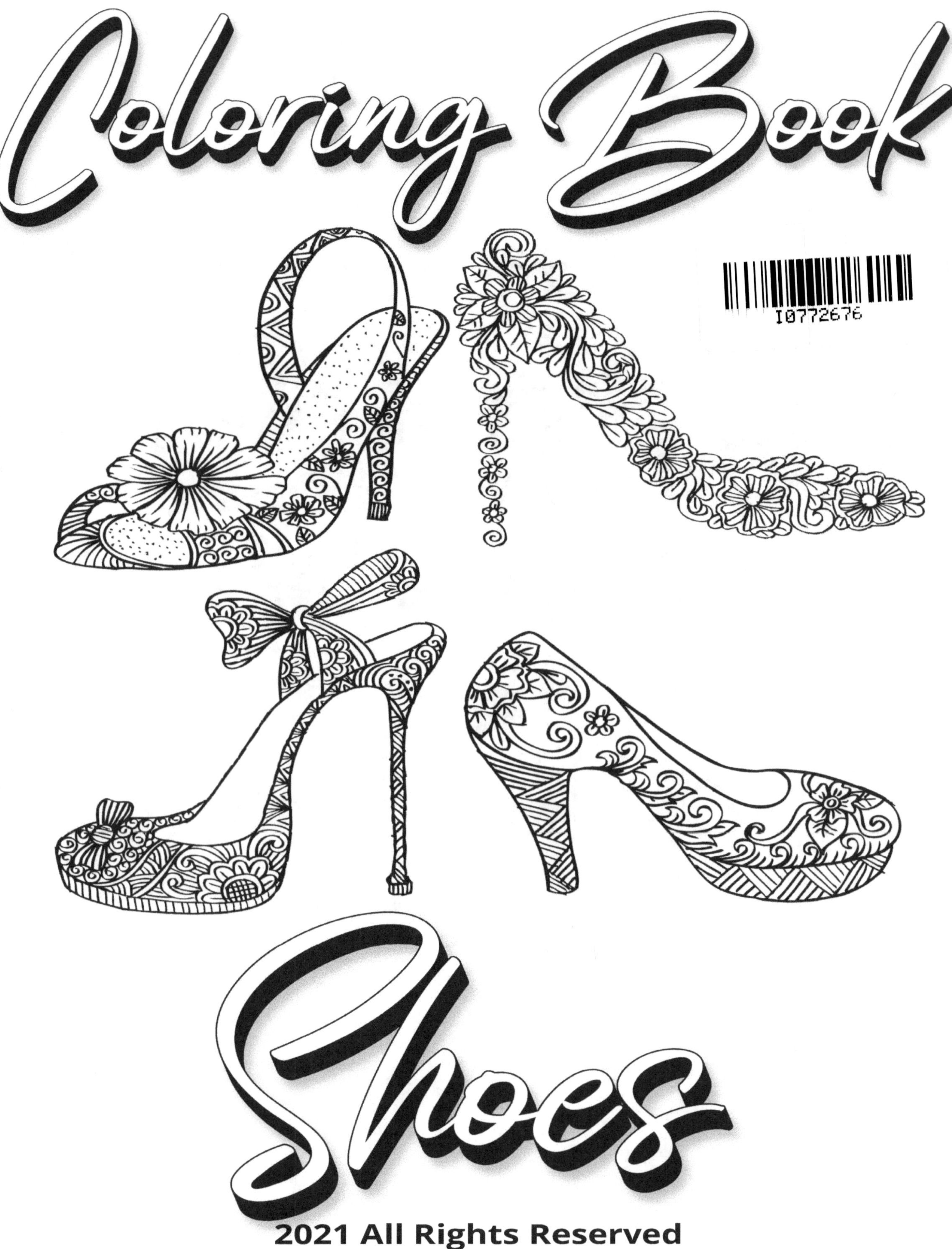

Shoes

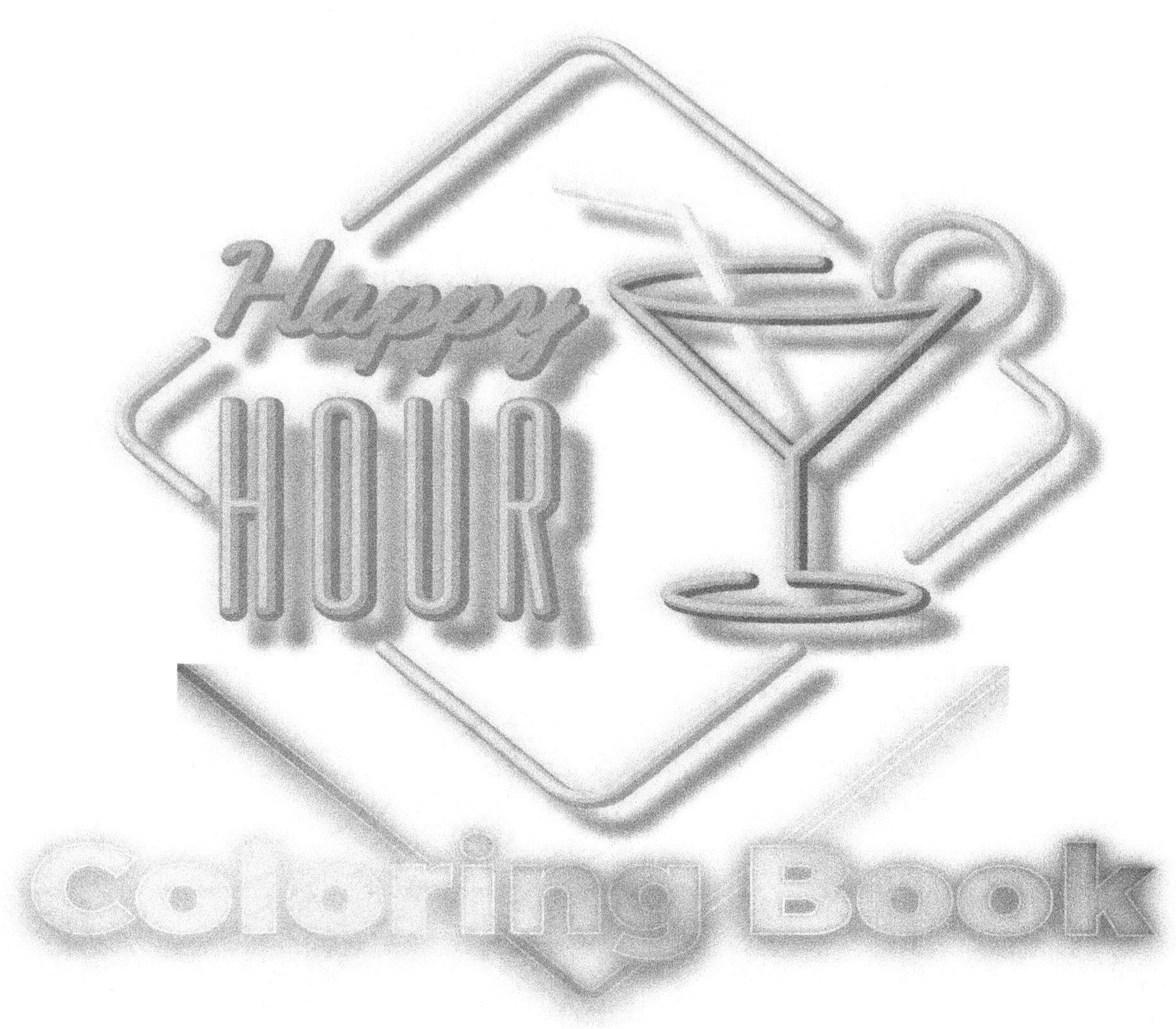
Happy
HOUR
Coloring Book

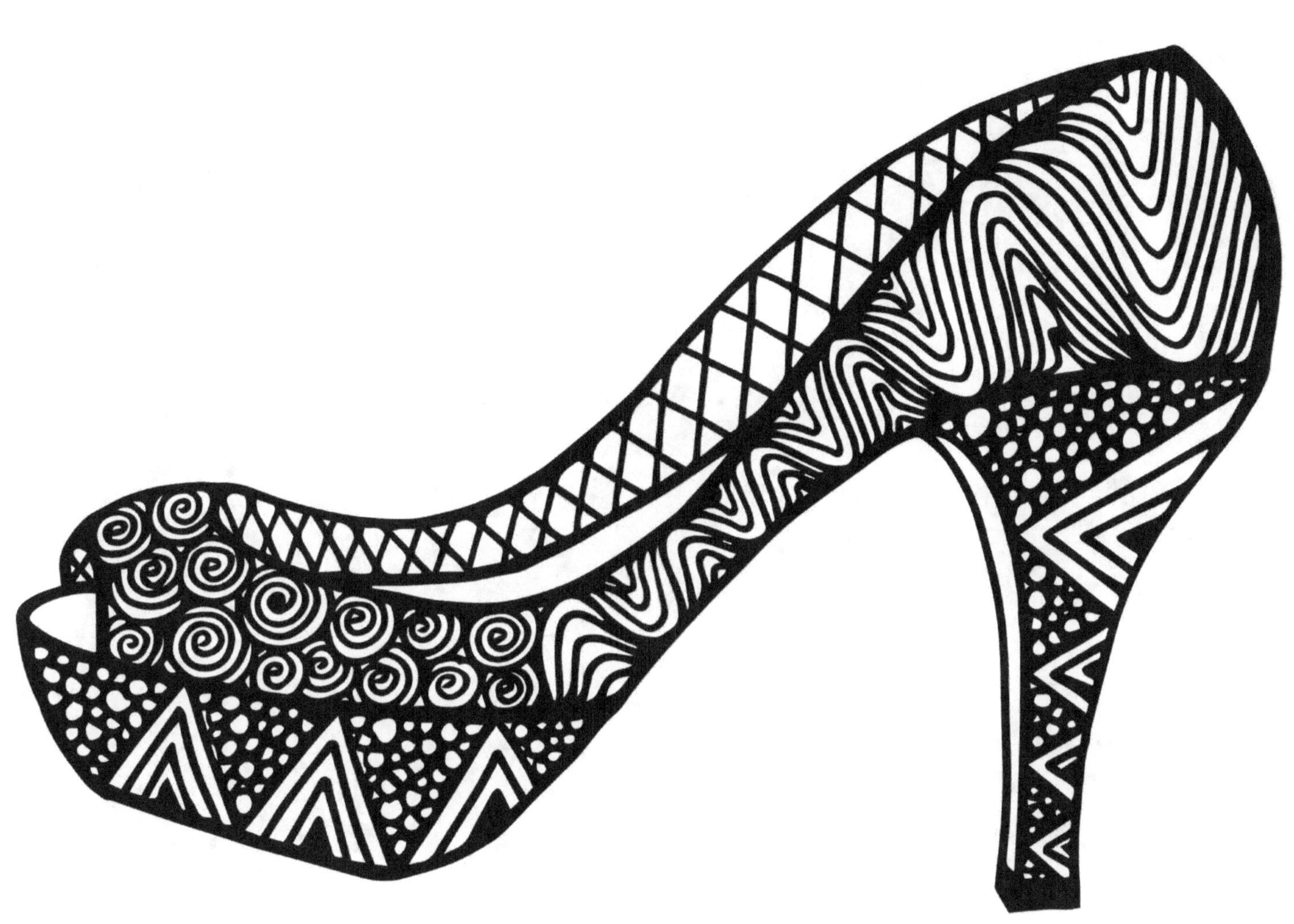

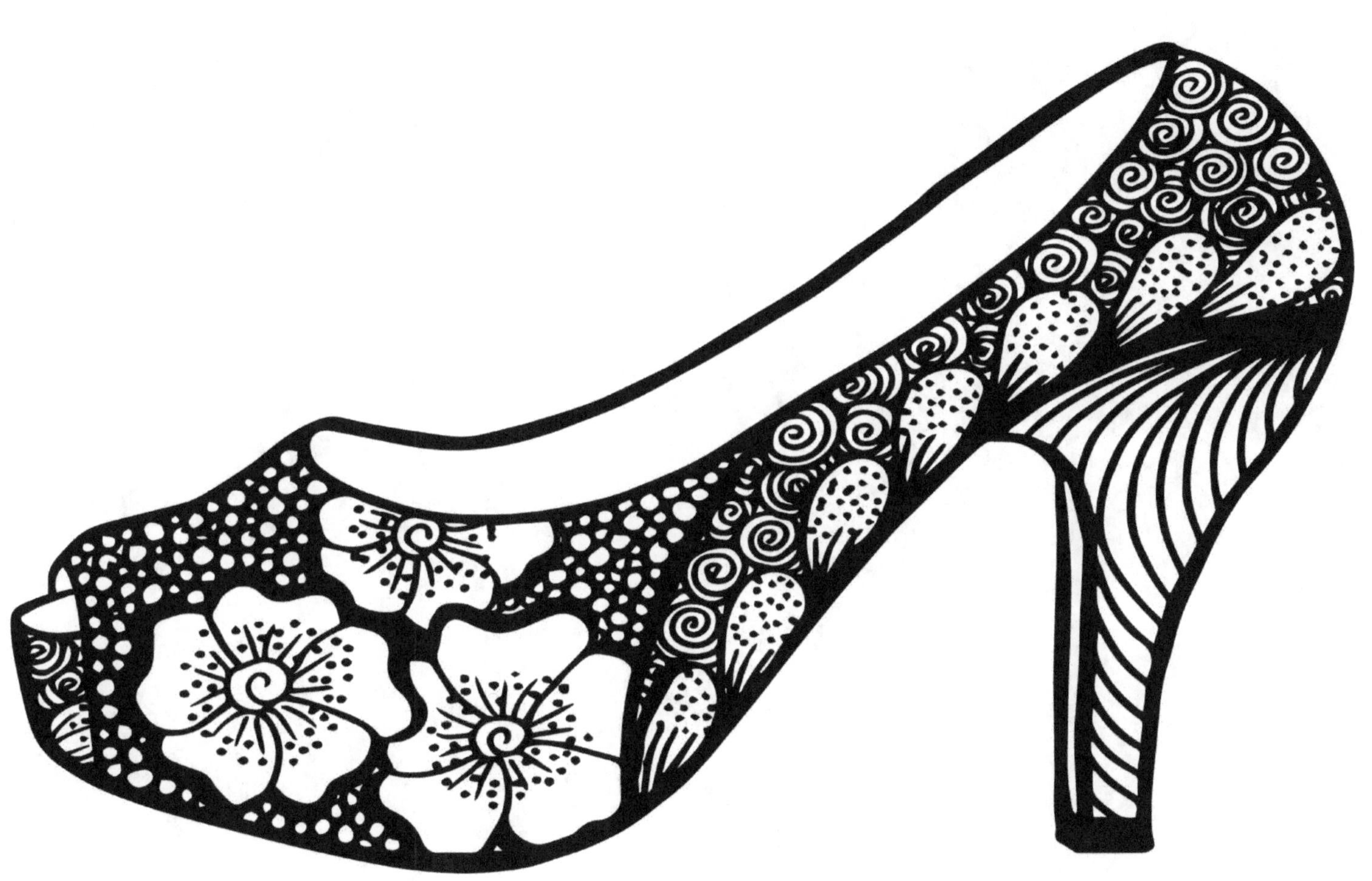

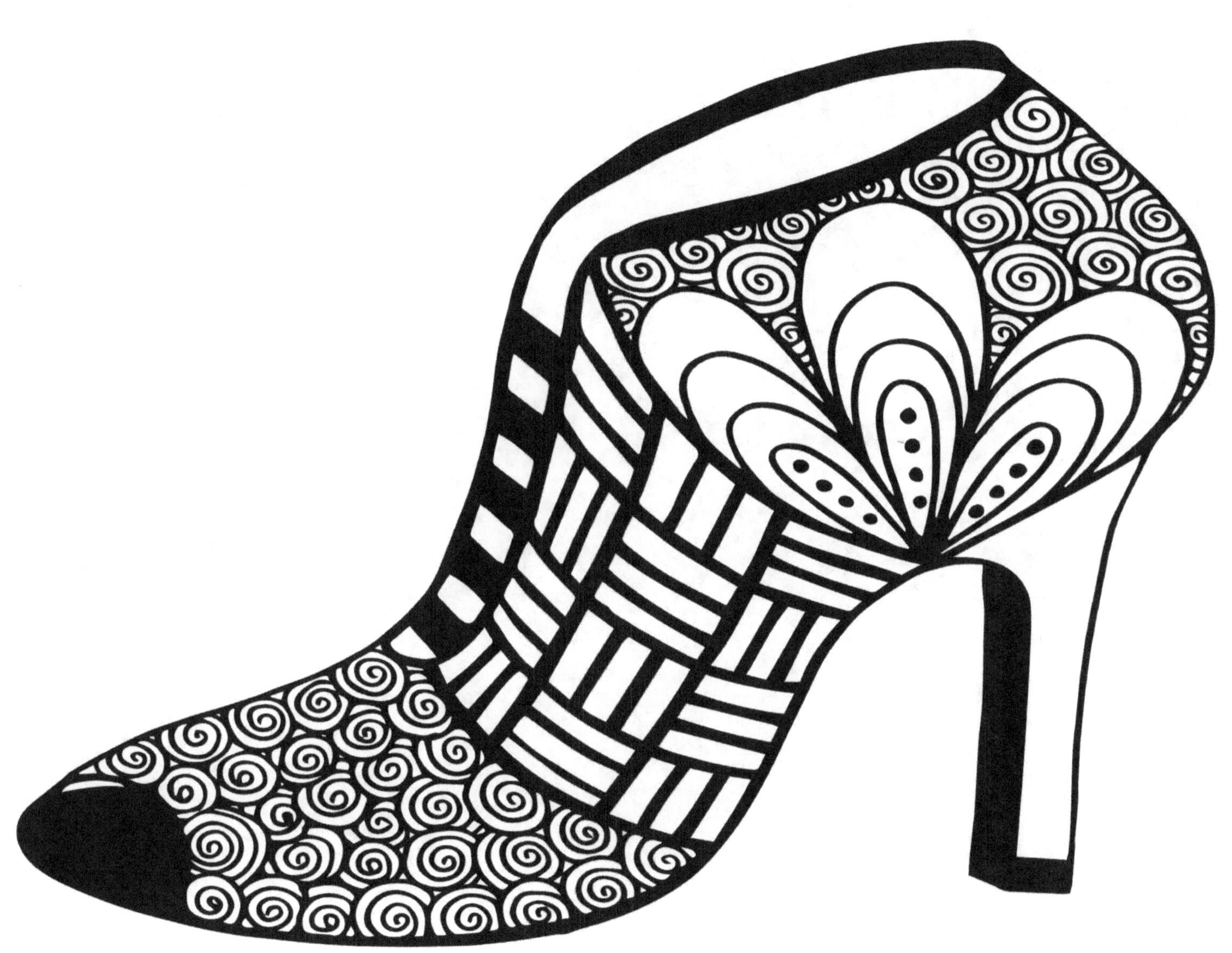

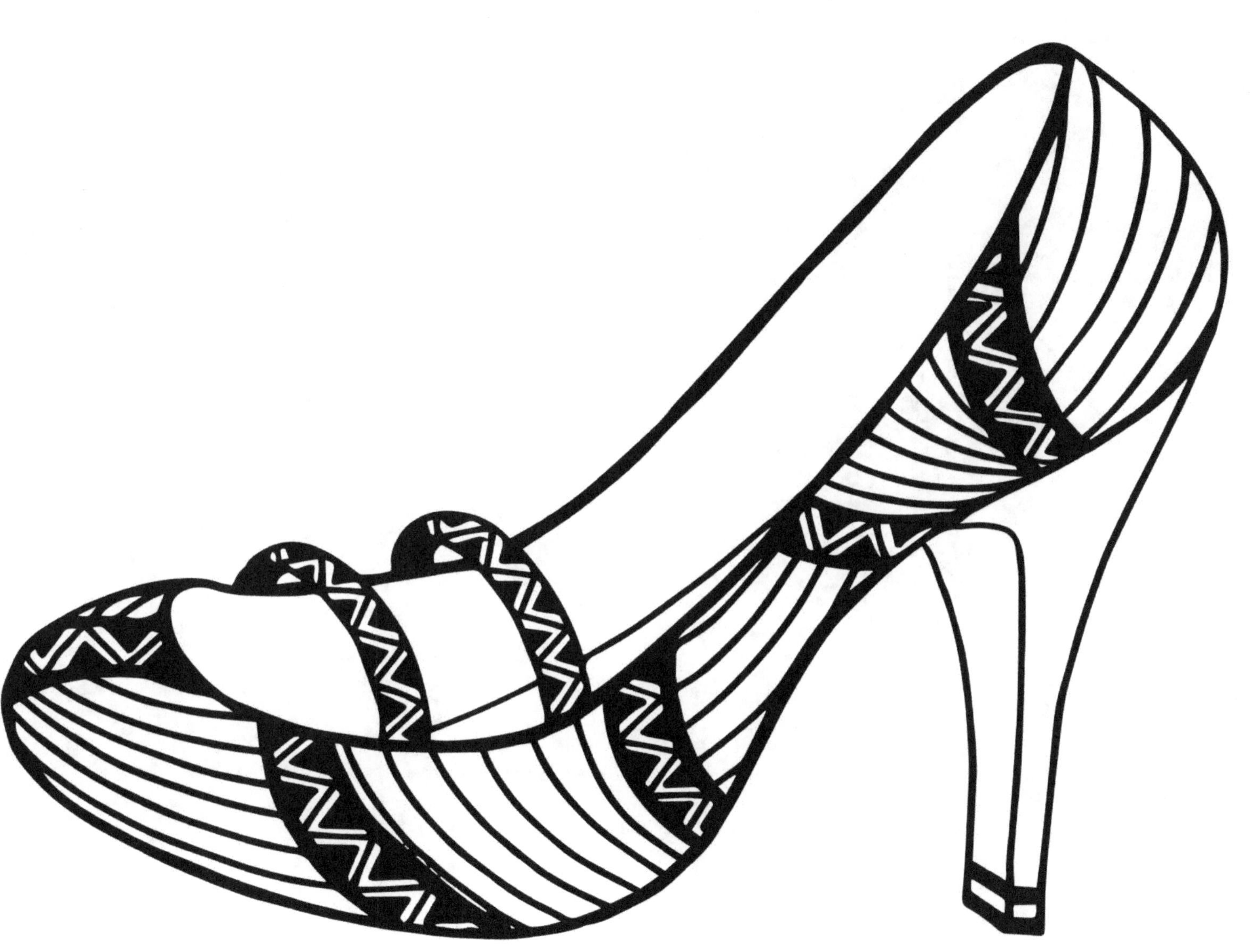

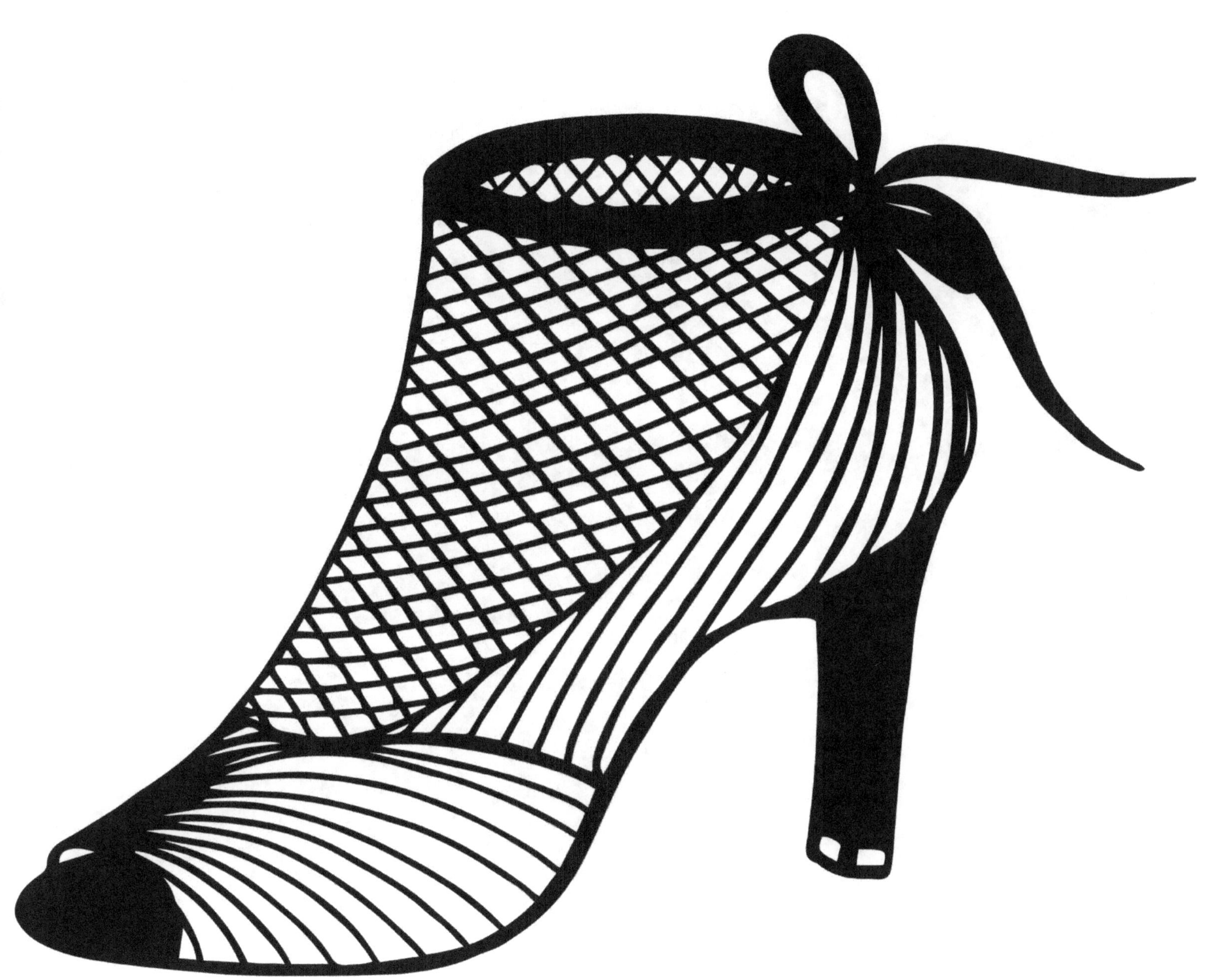

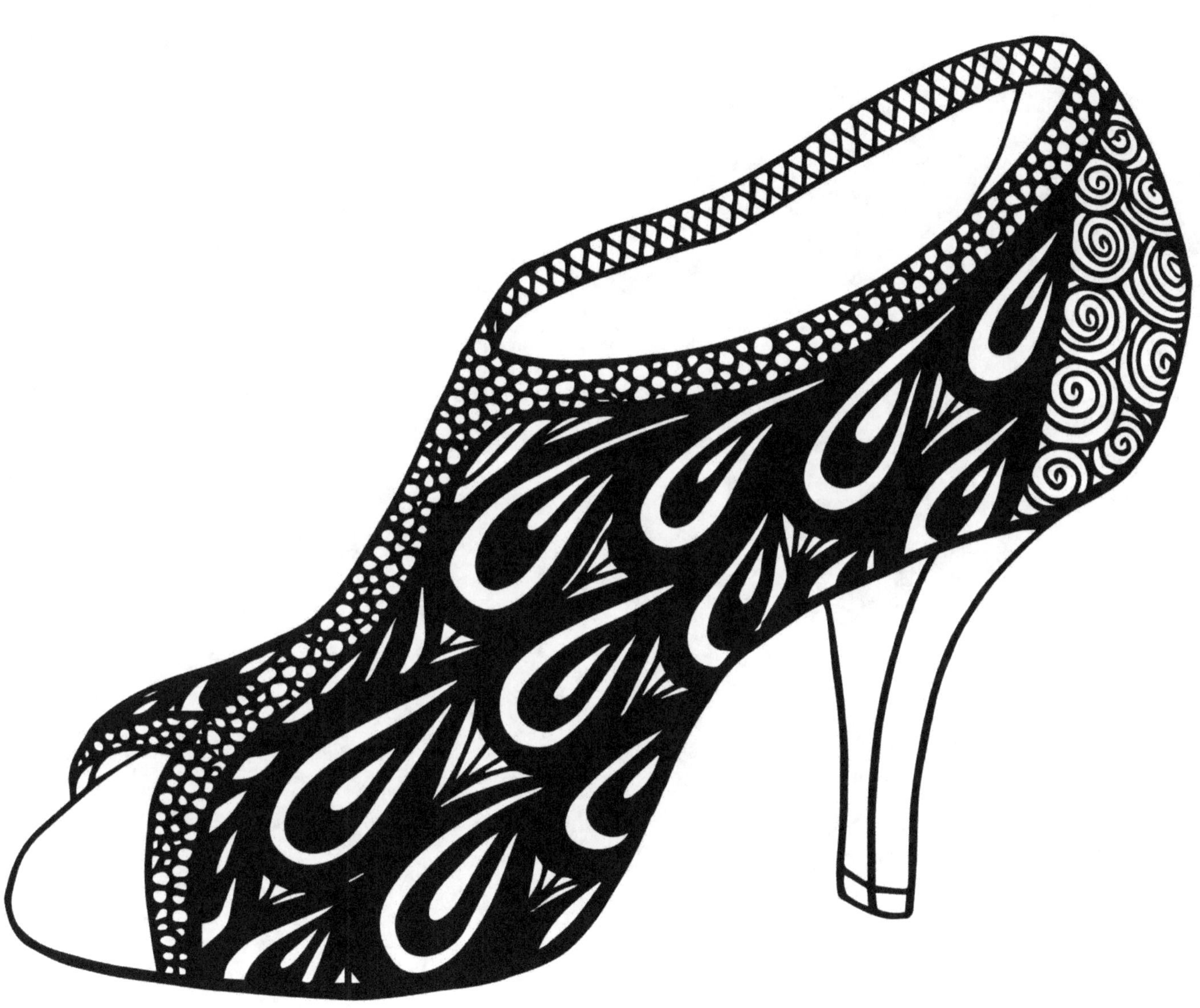

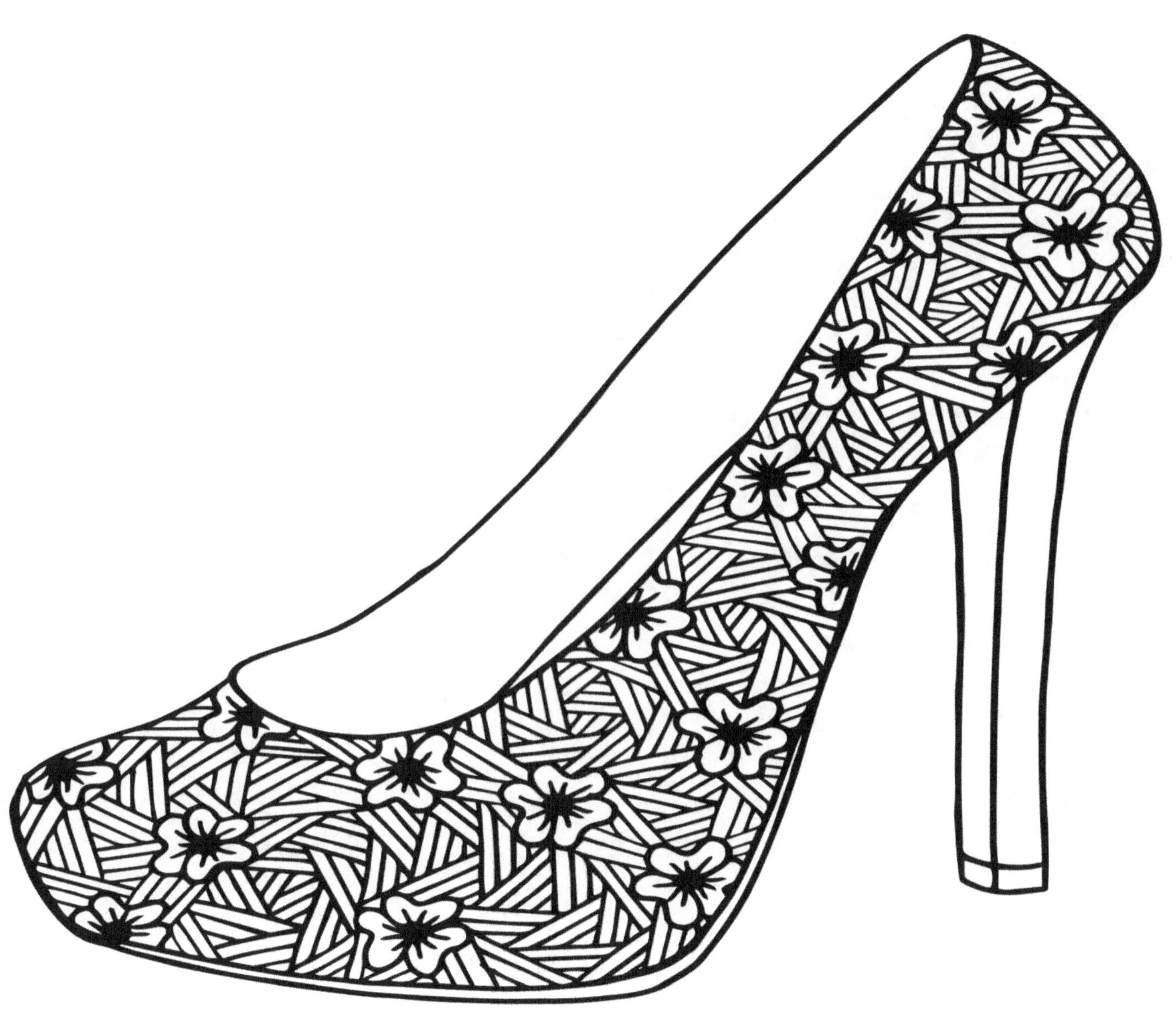

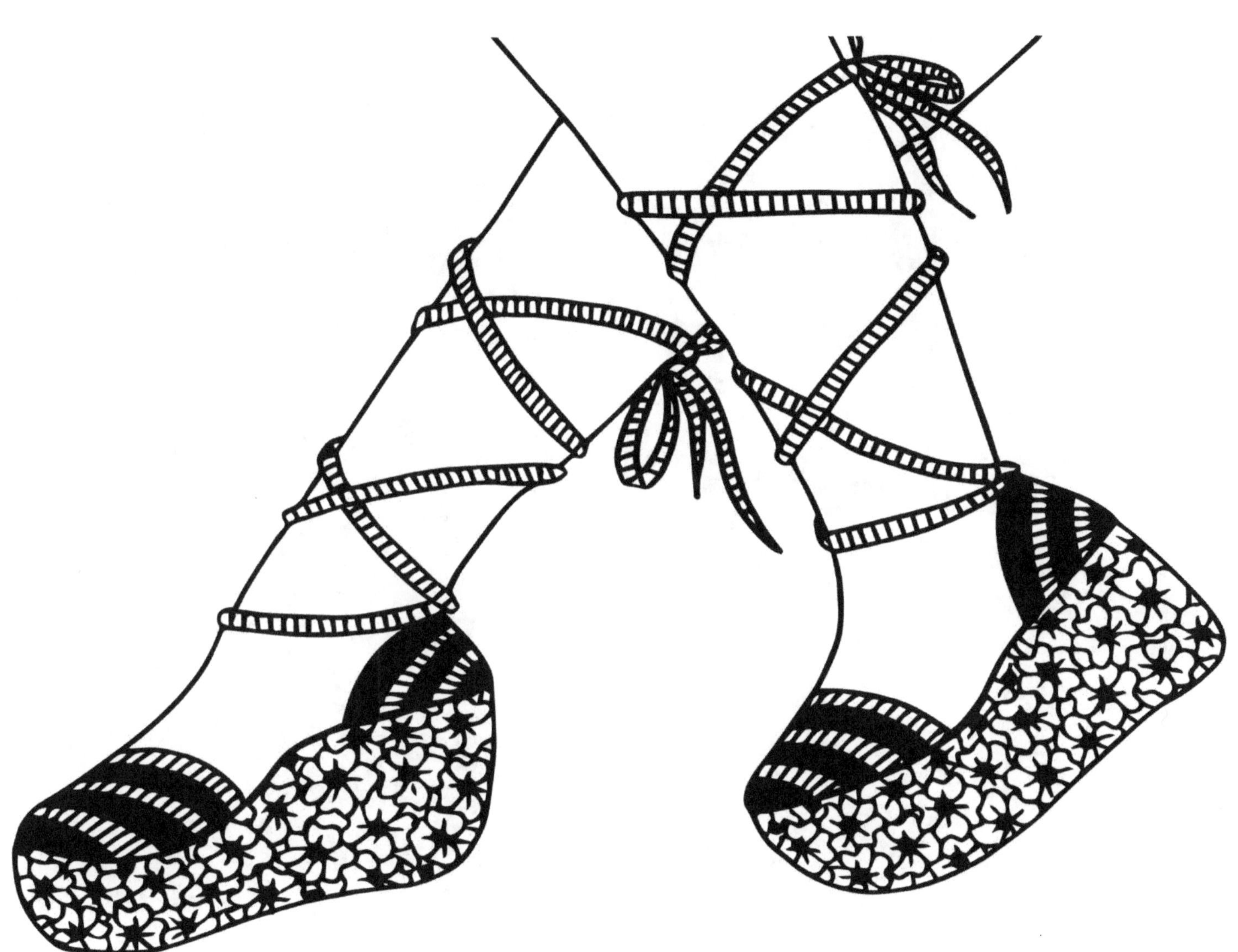

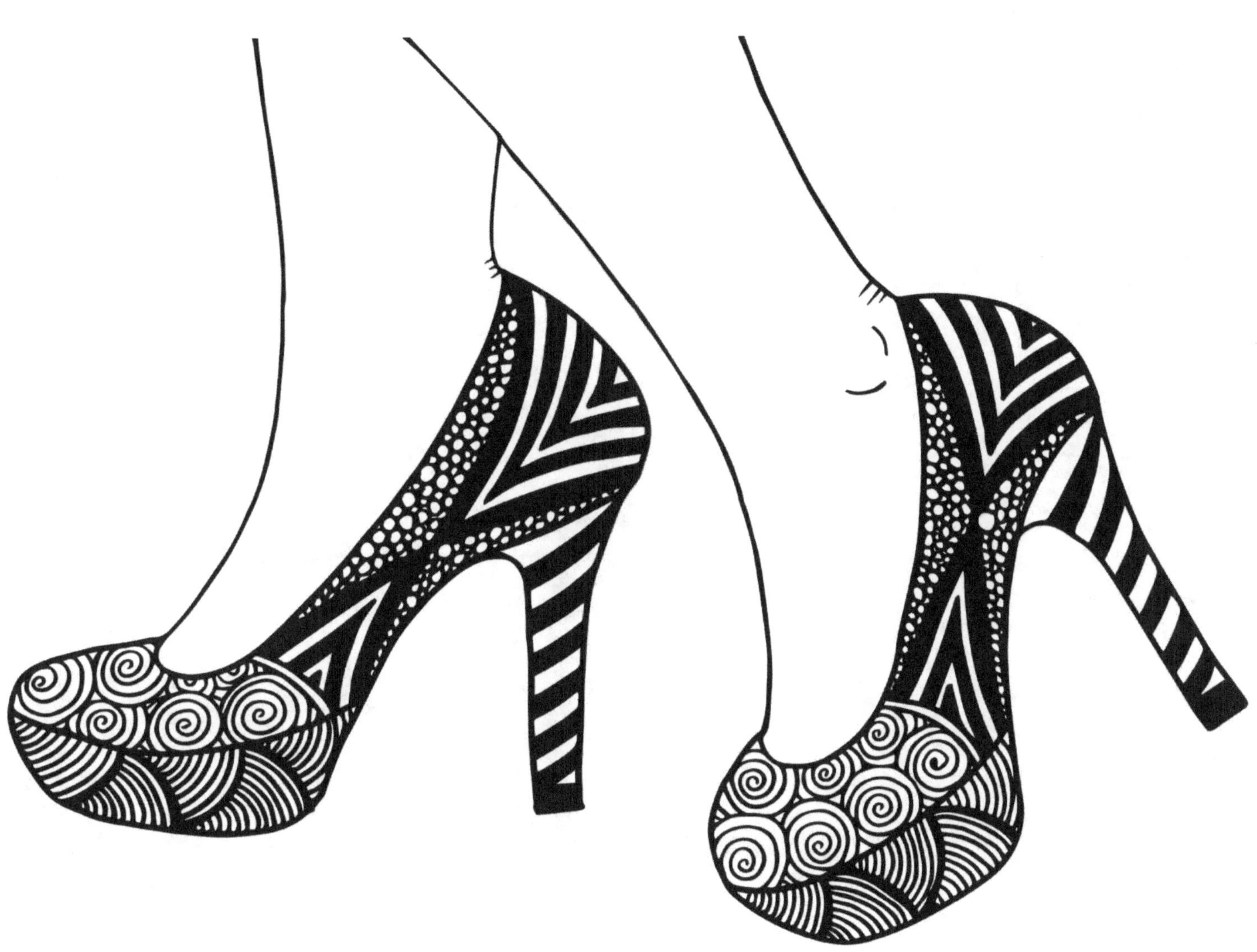

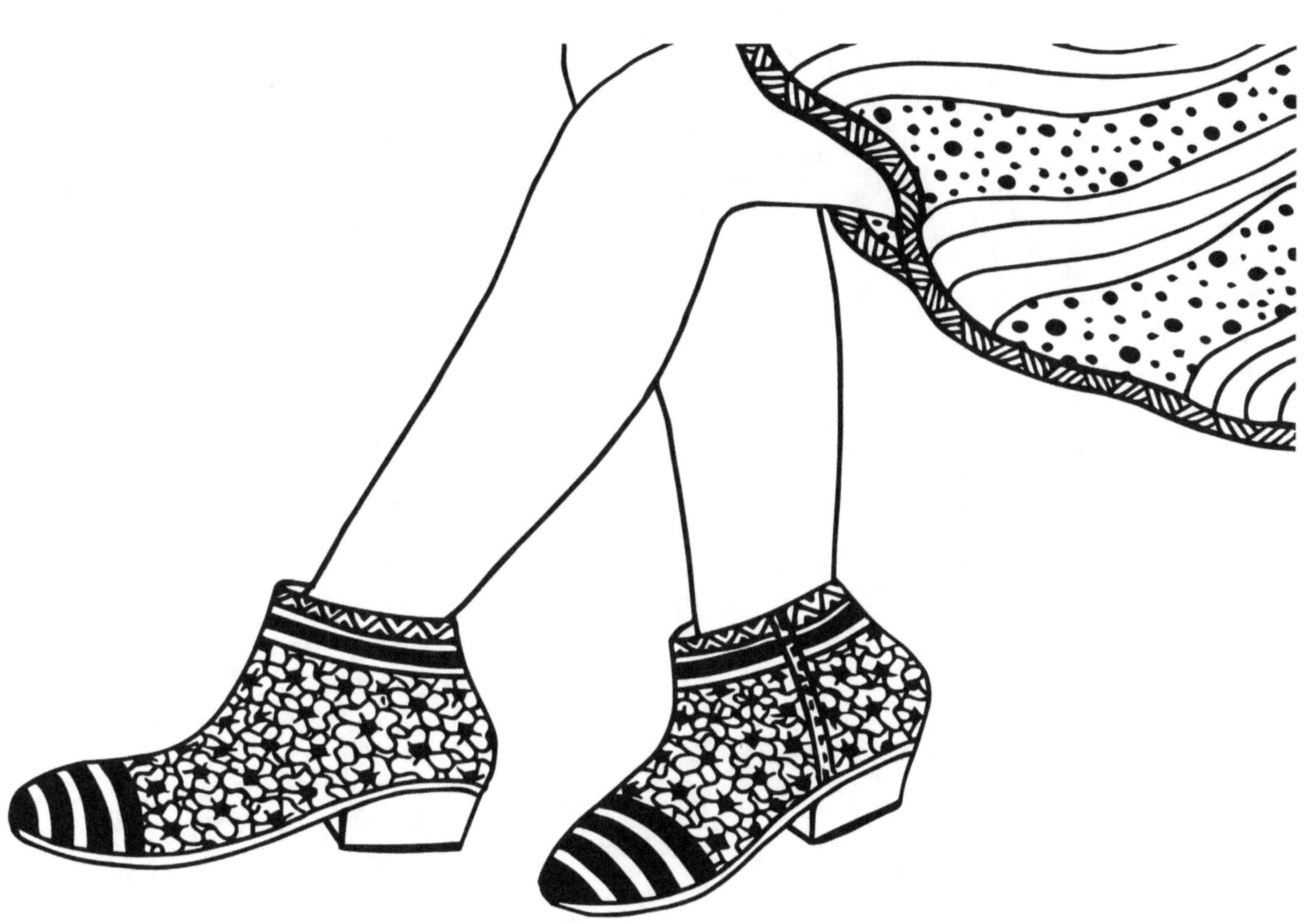

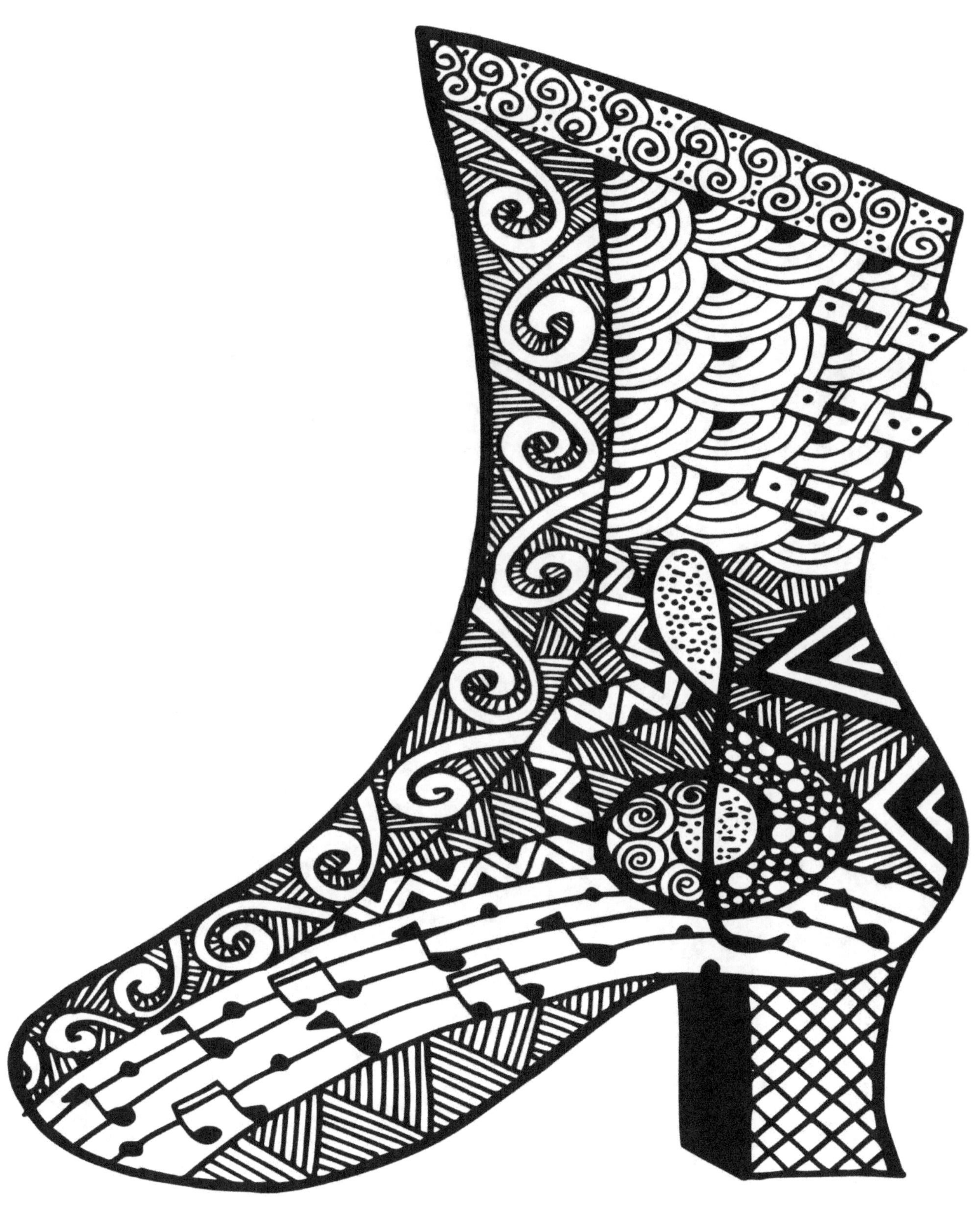

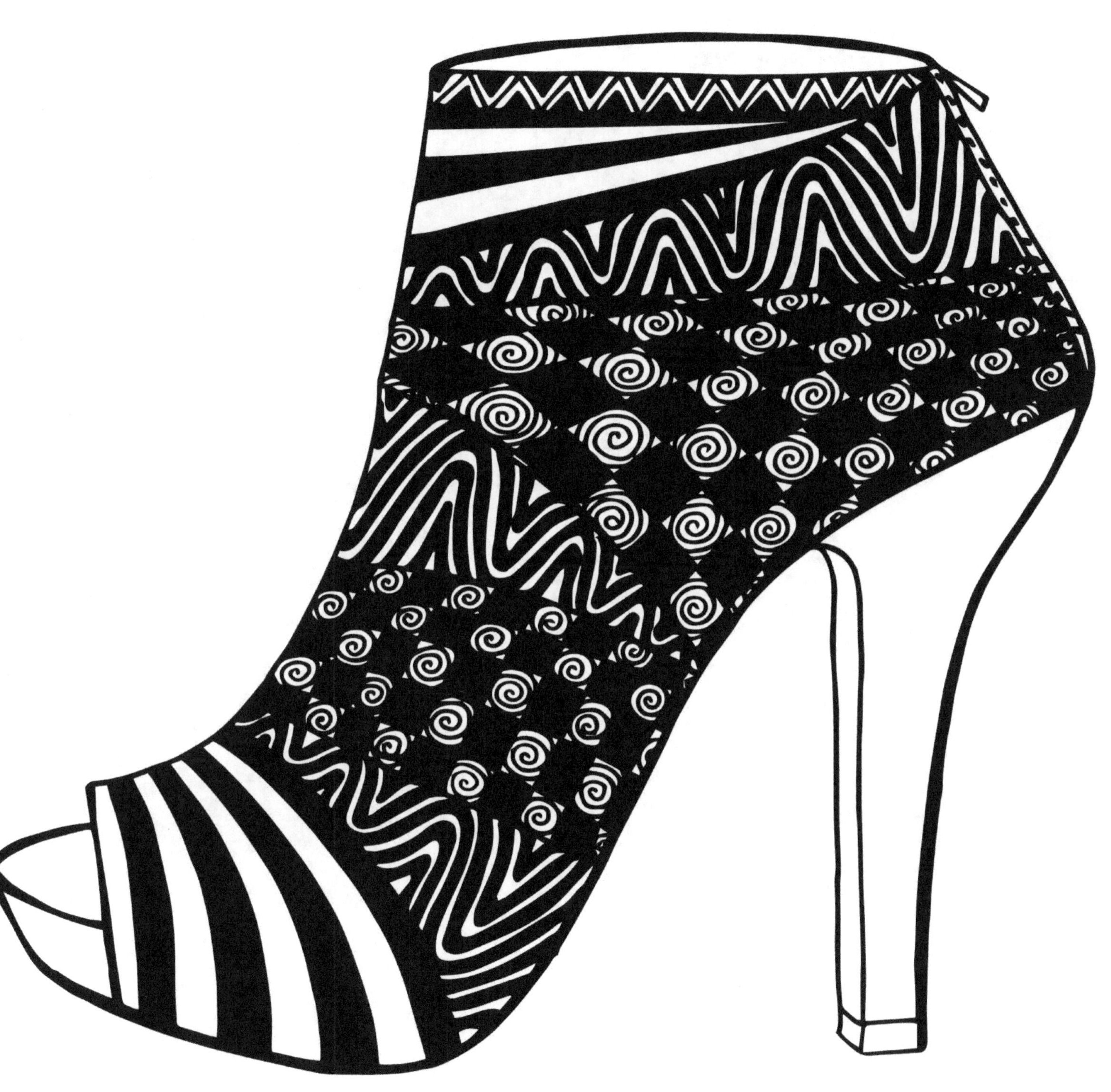

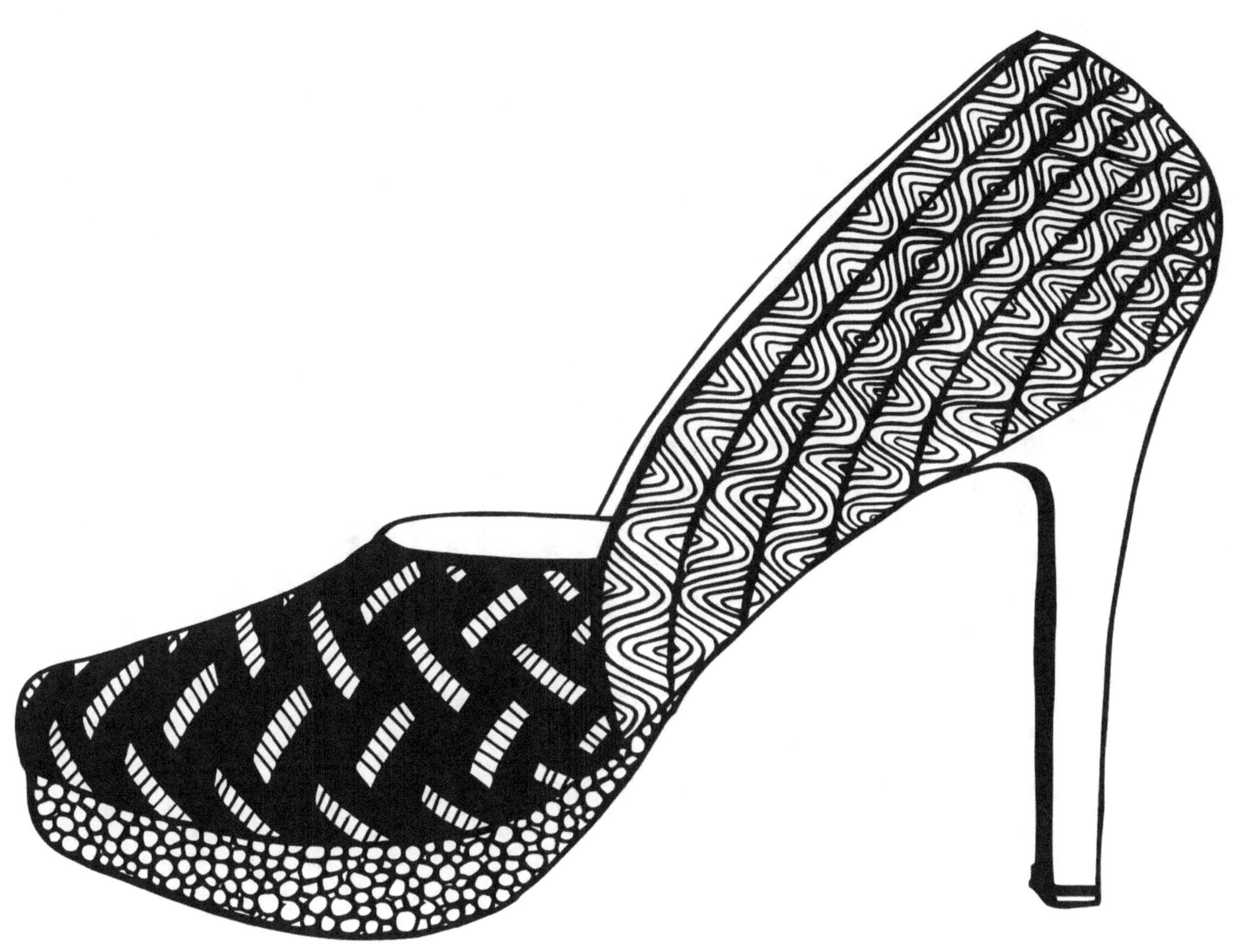

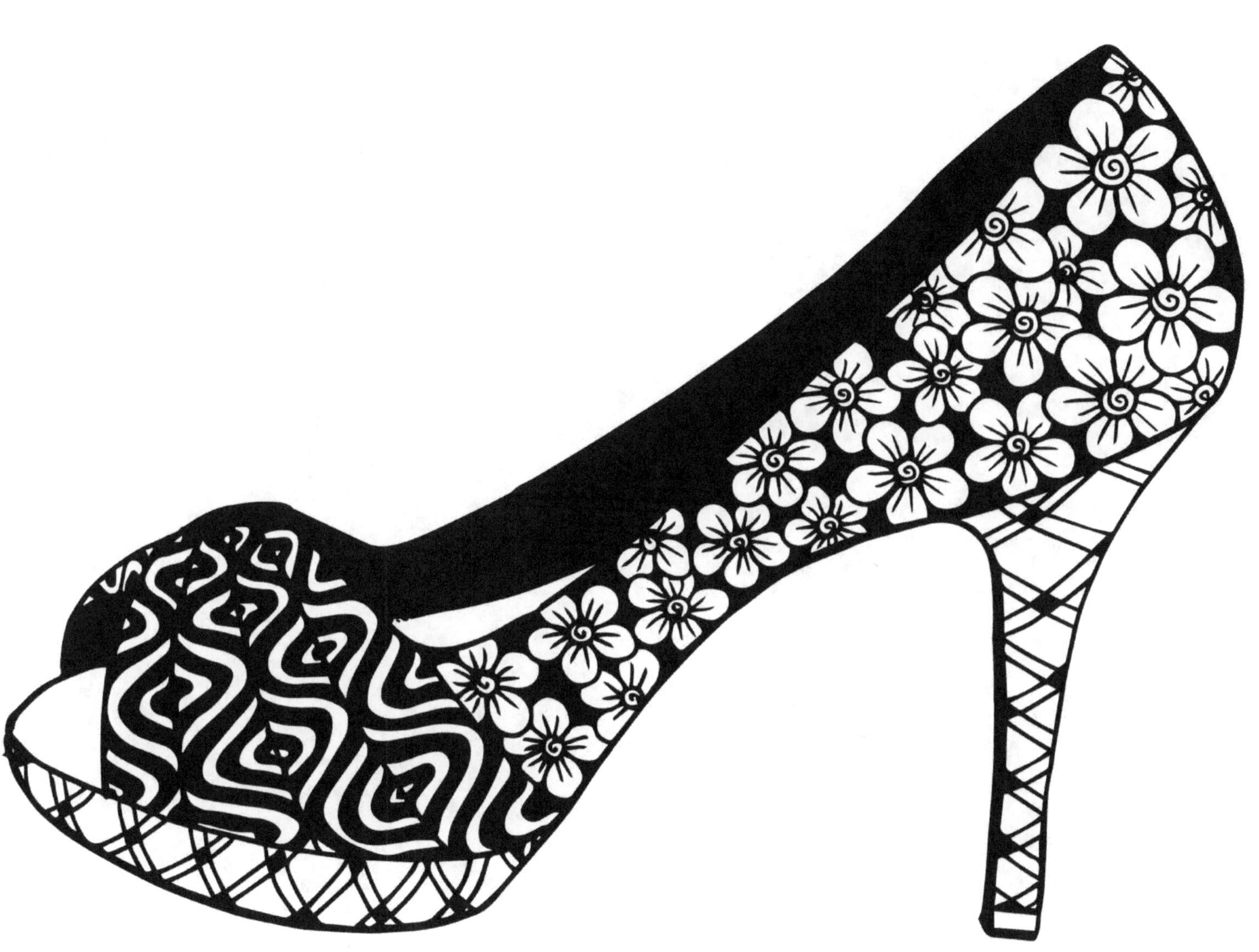

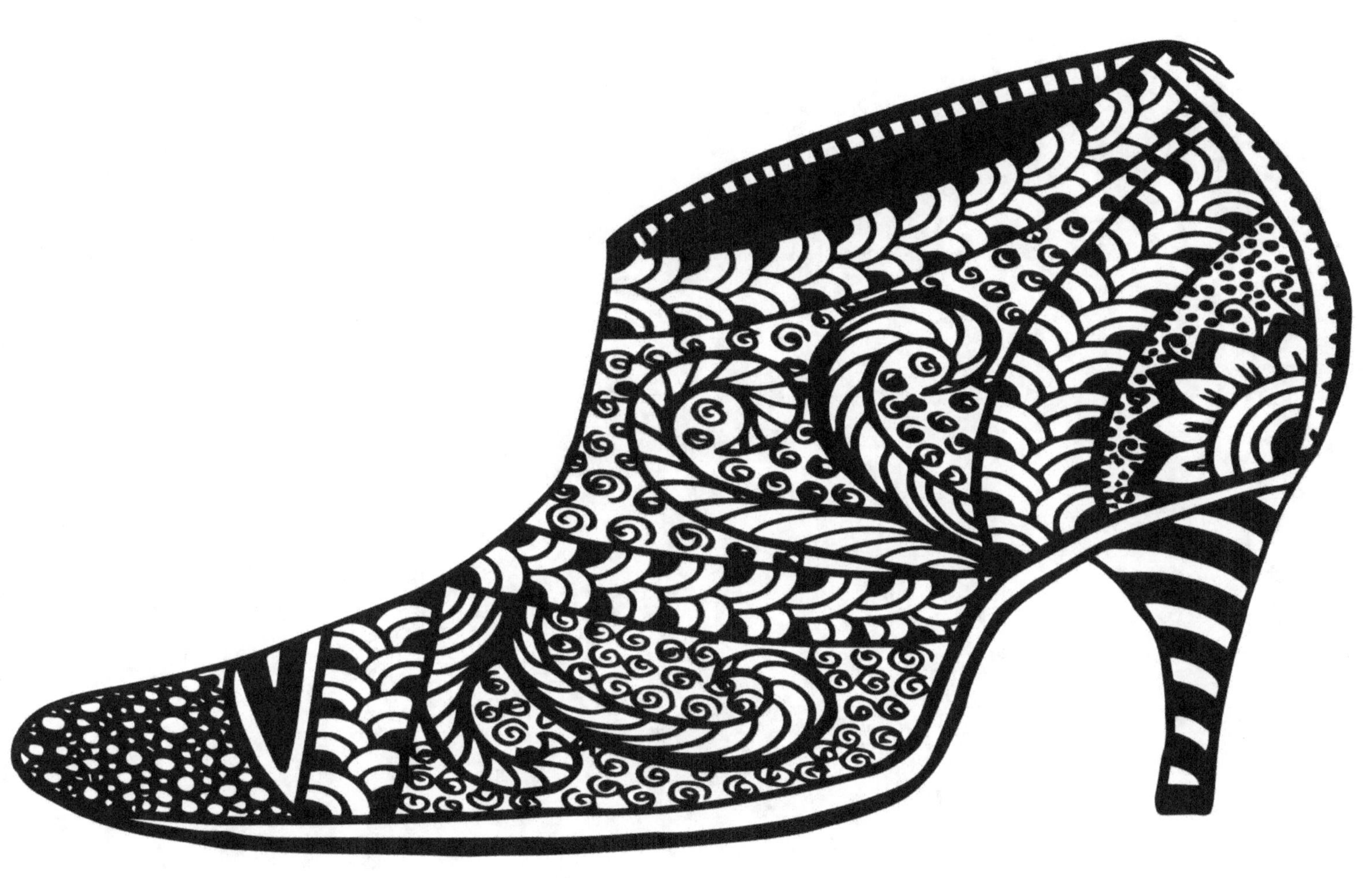

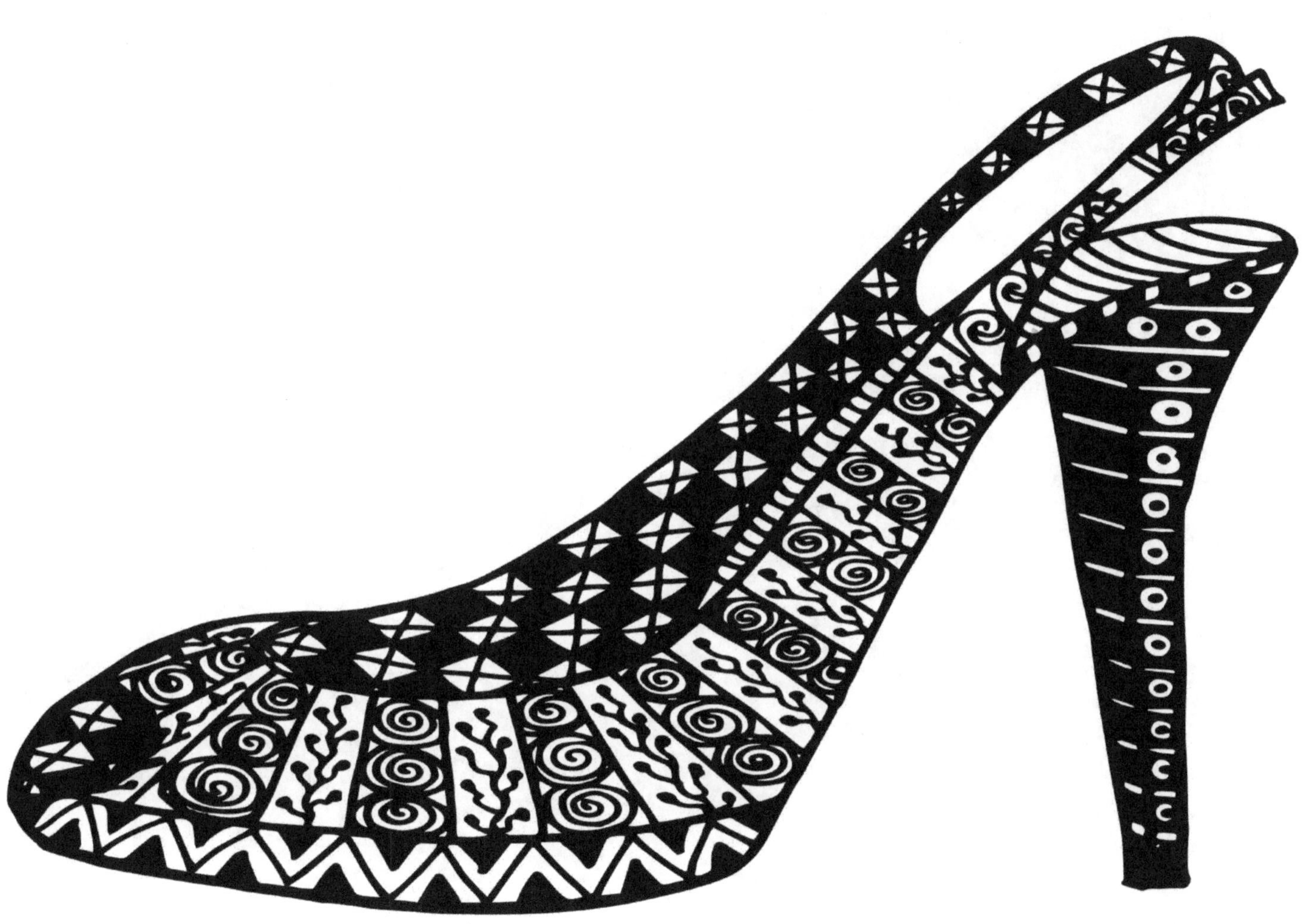

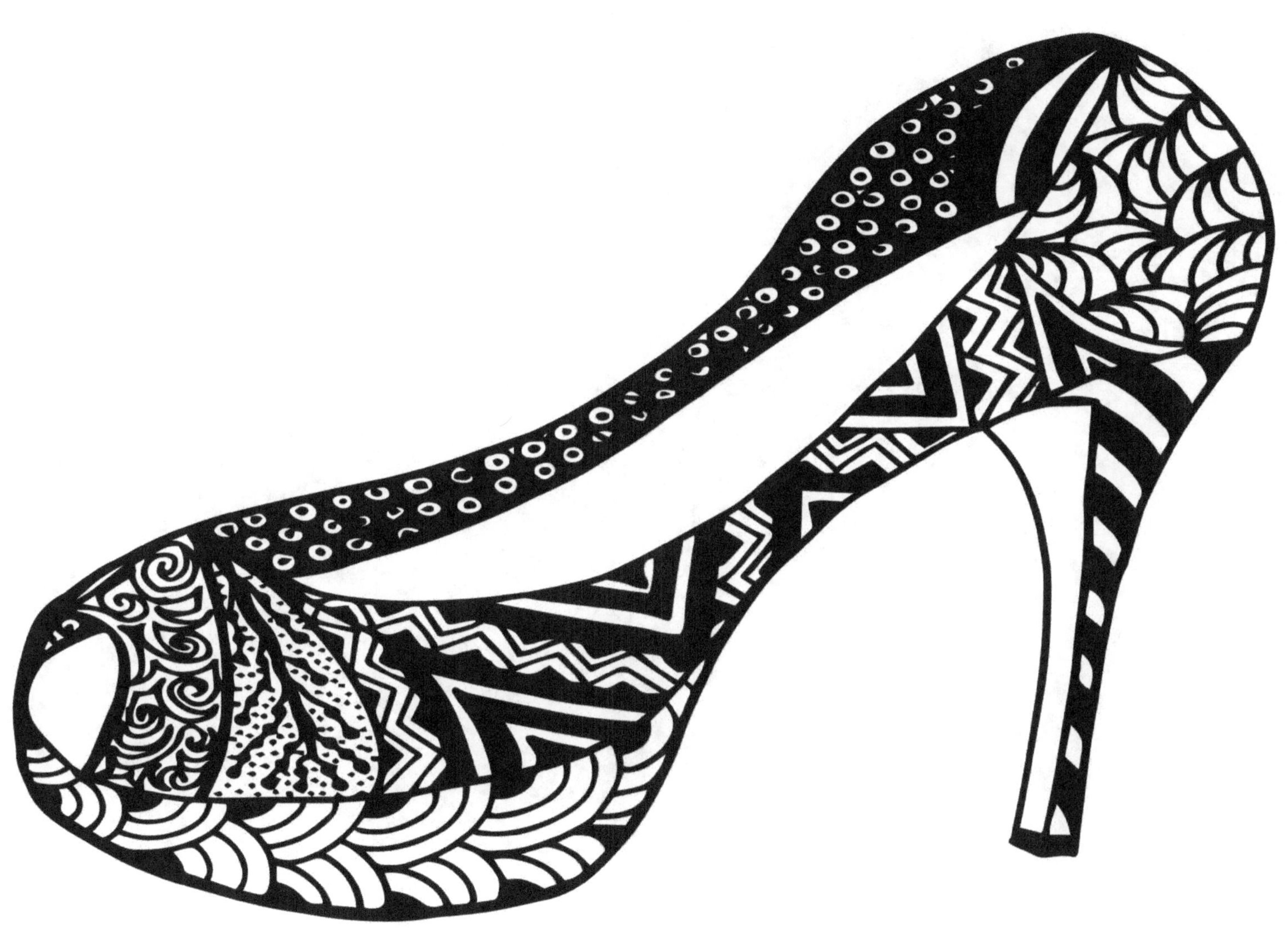

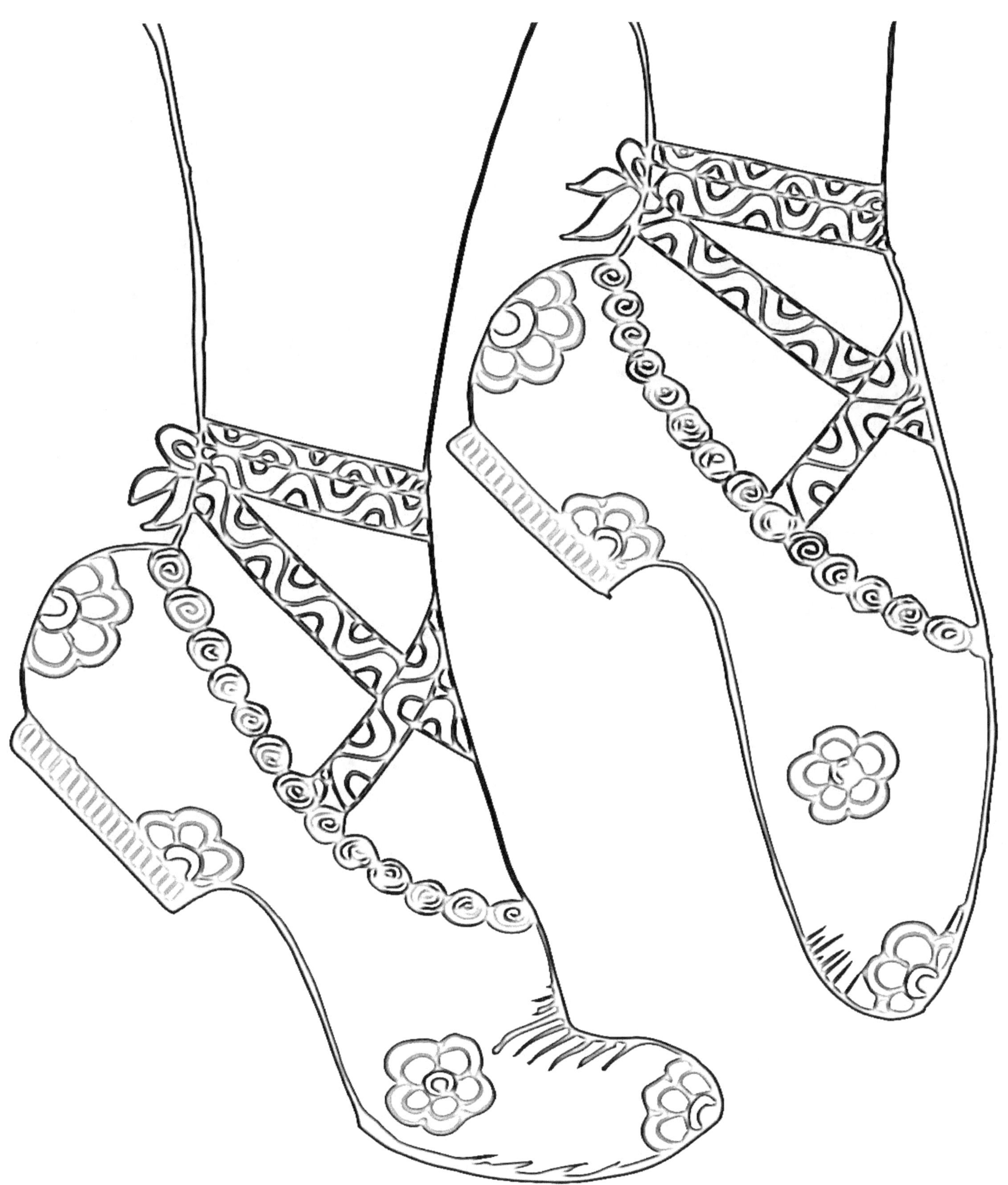

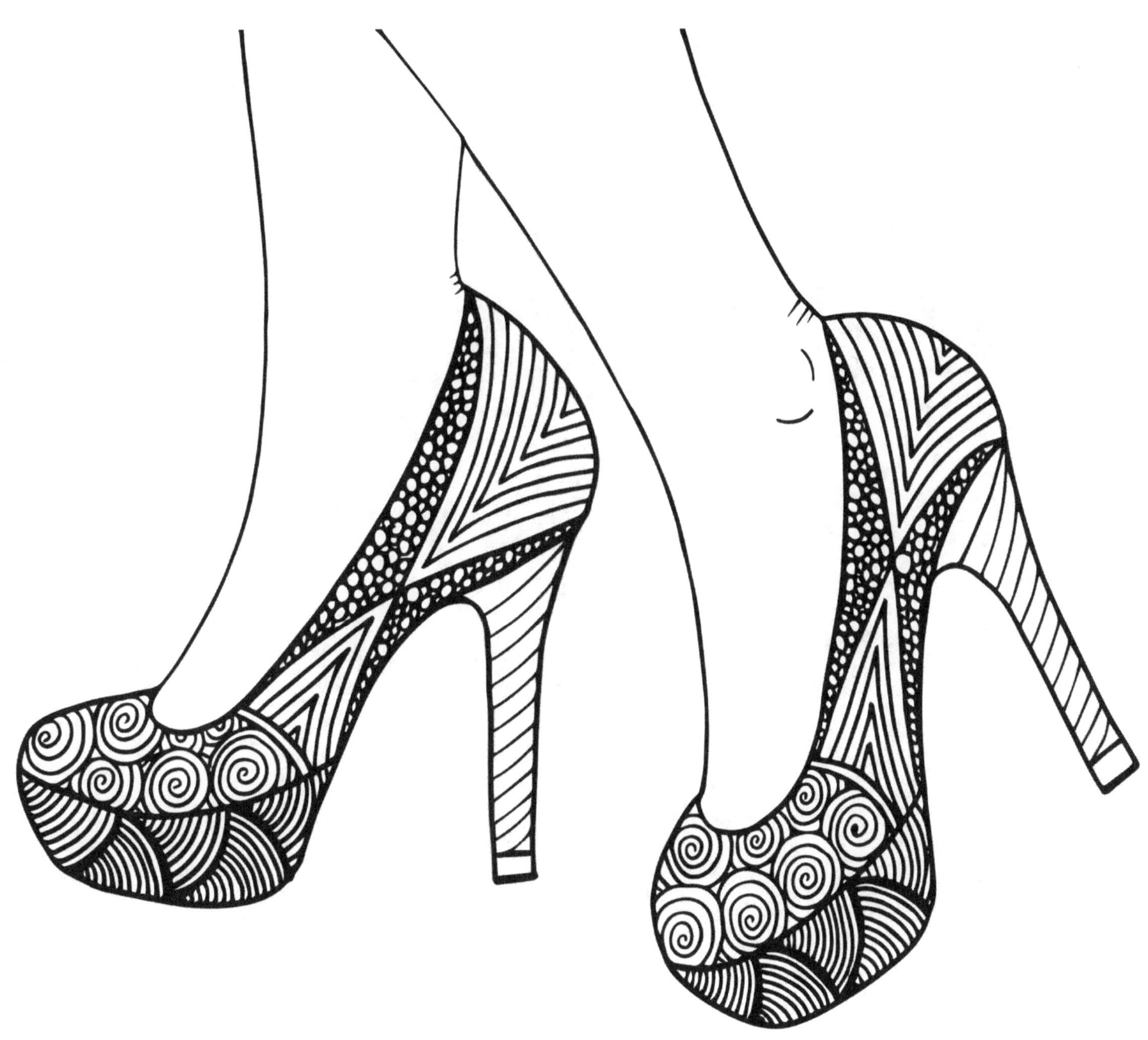

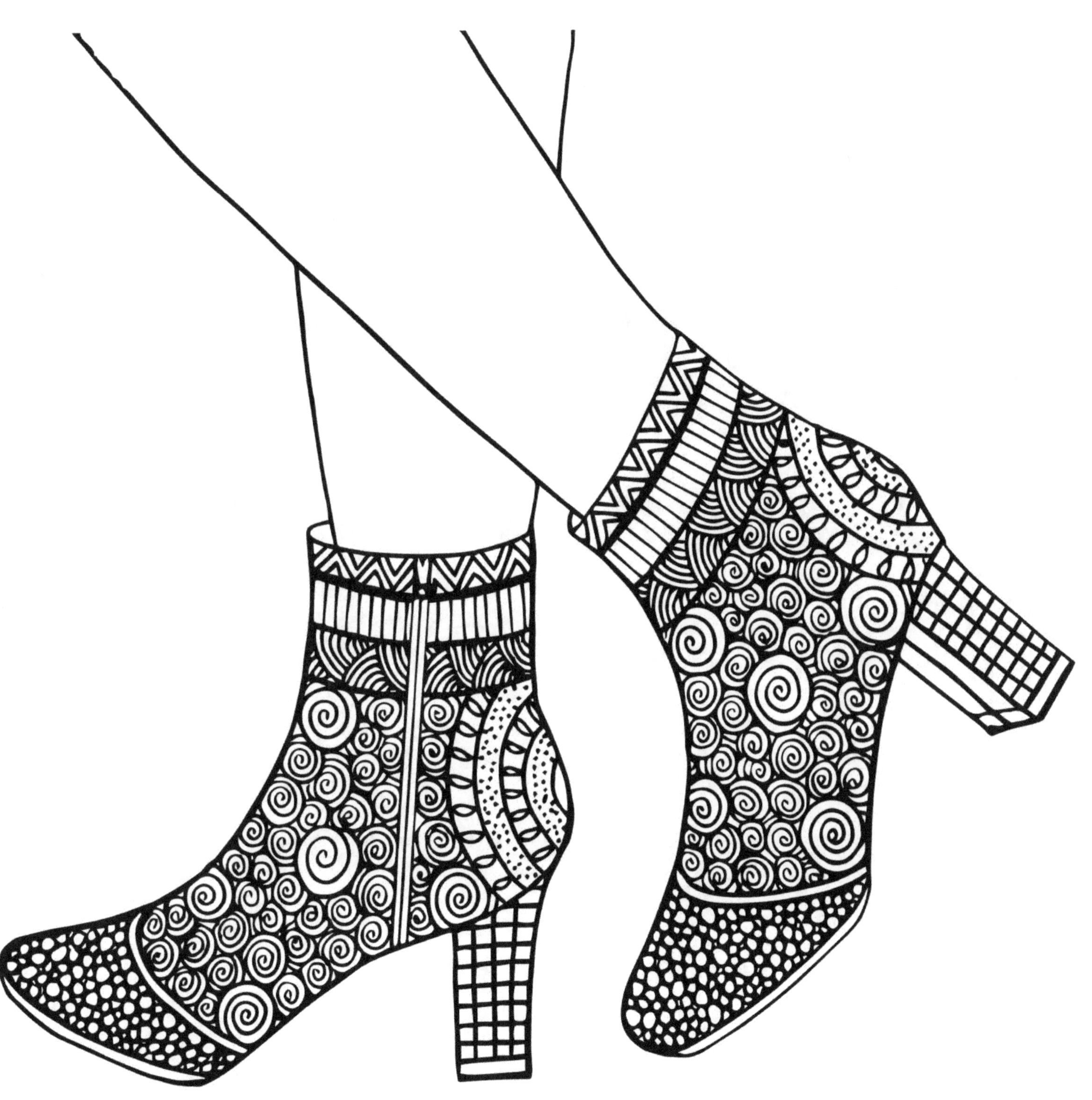

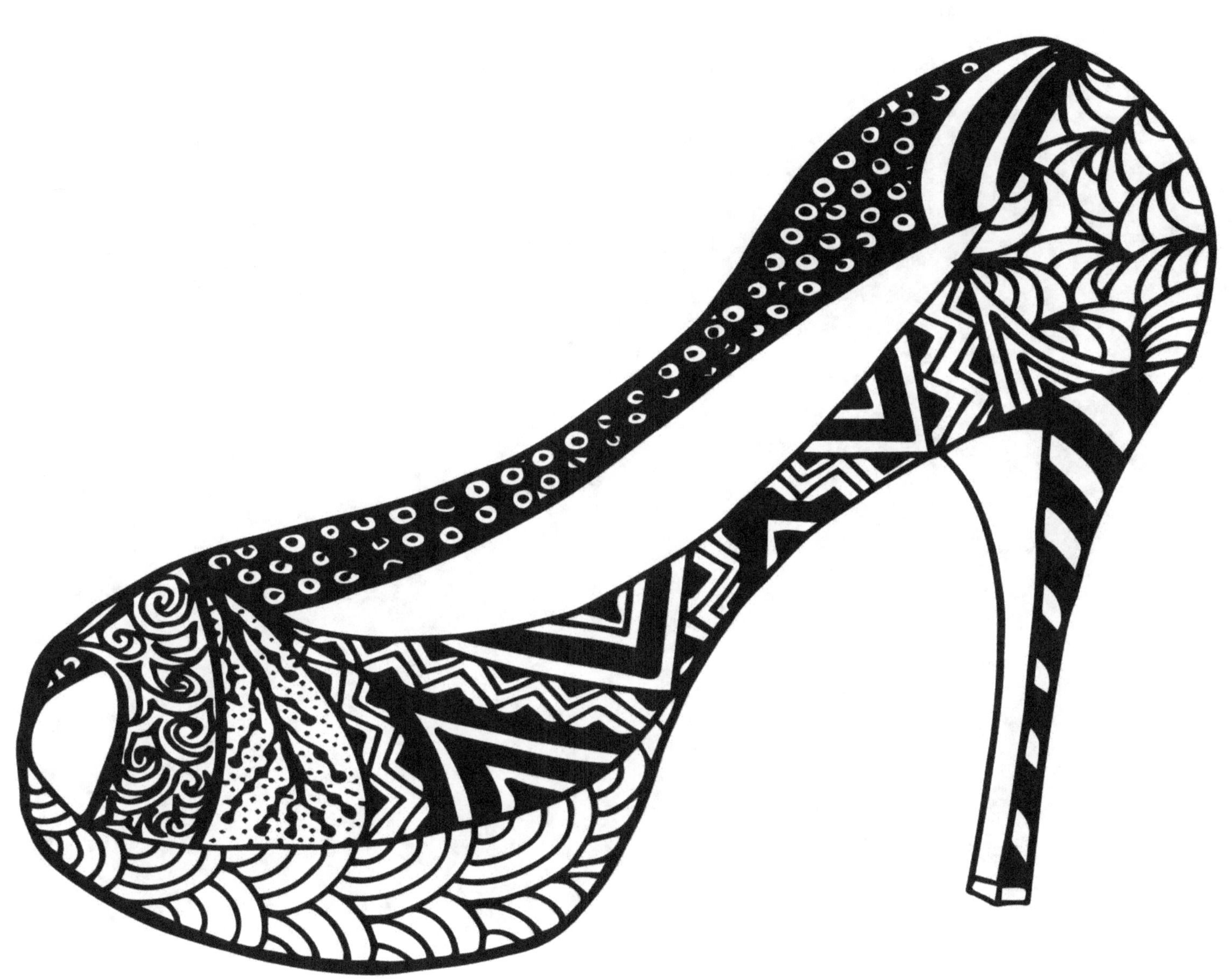

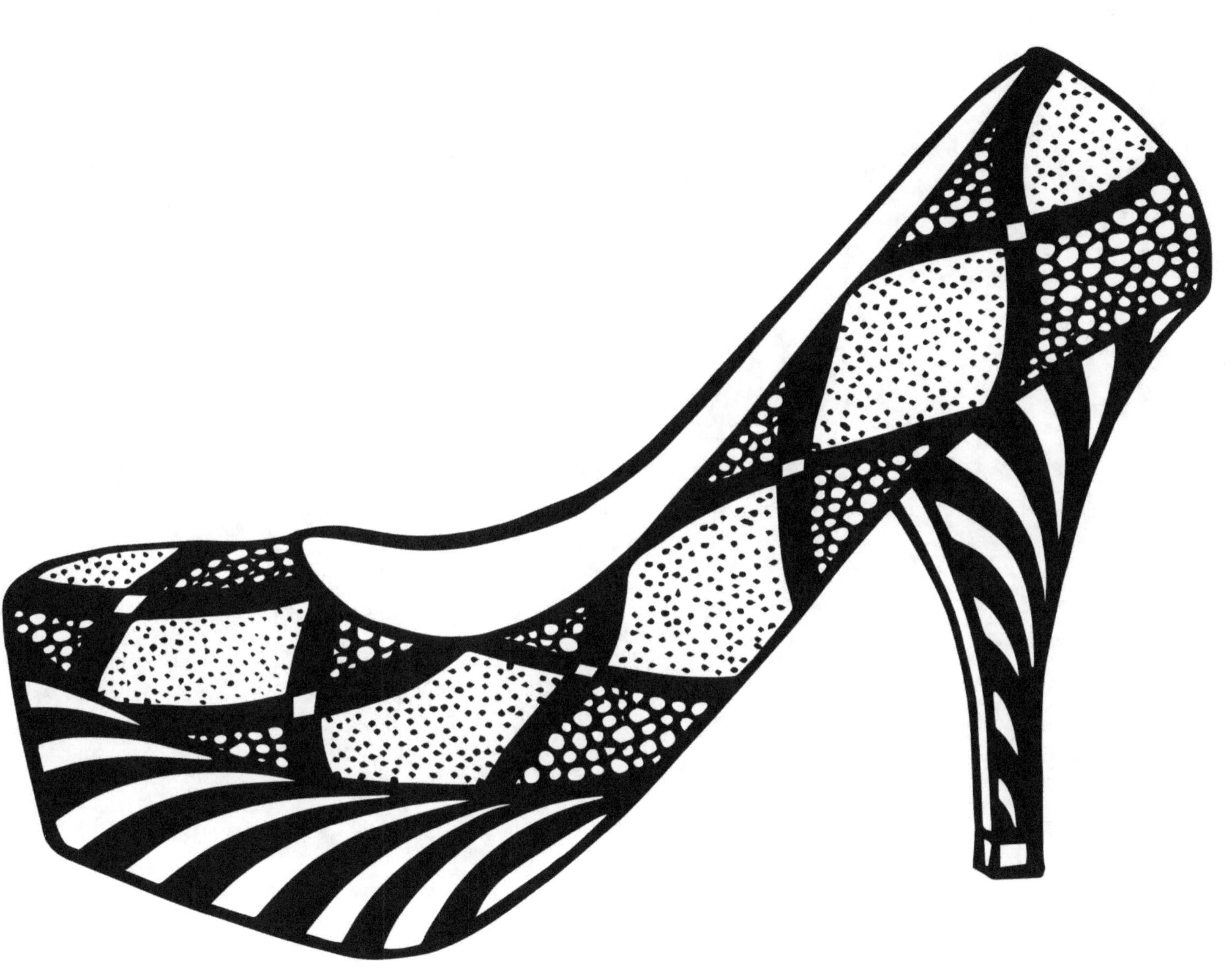

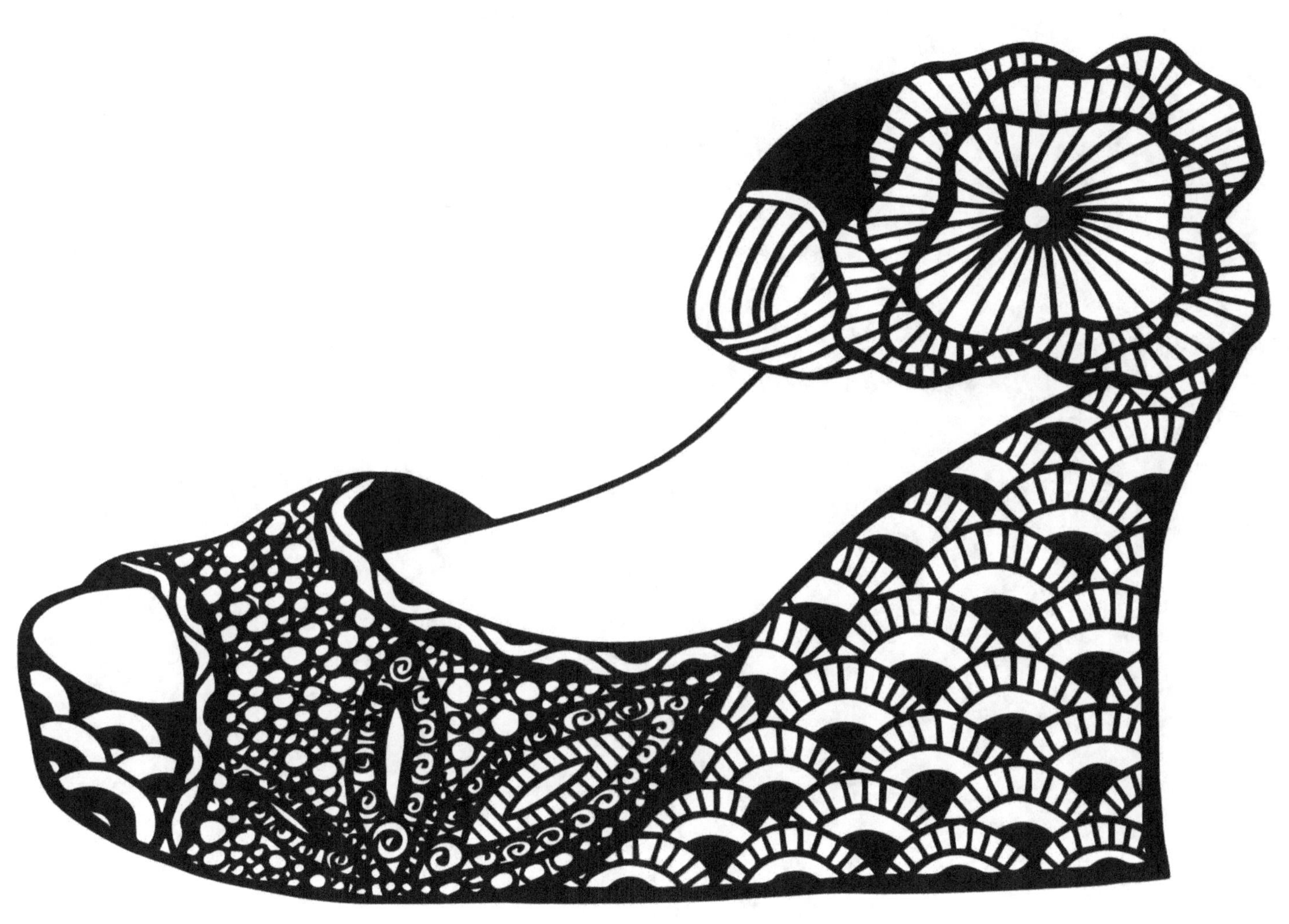

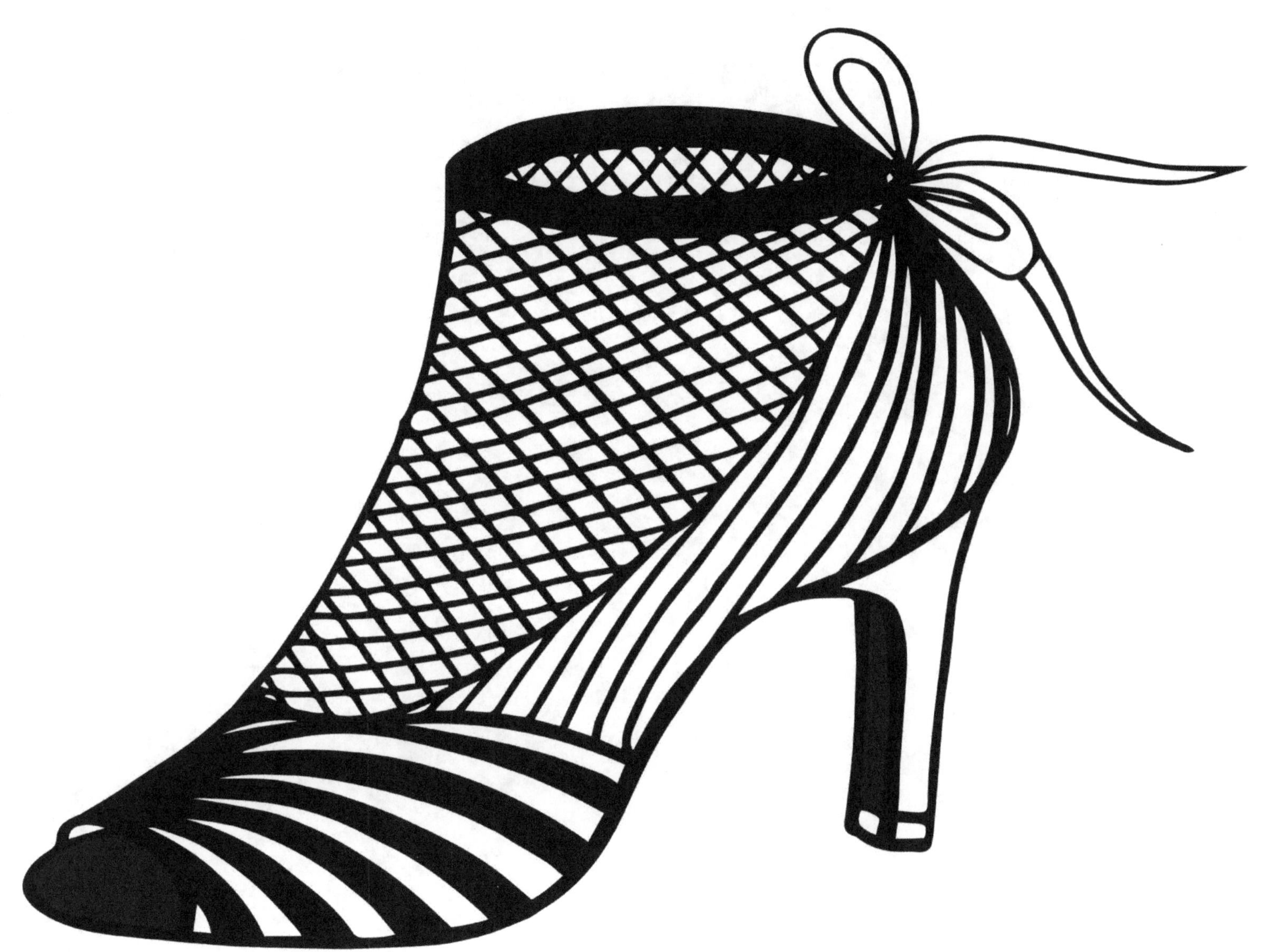

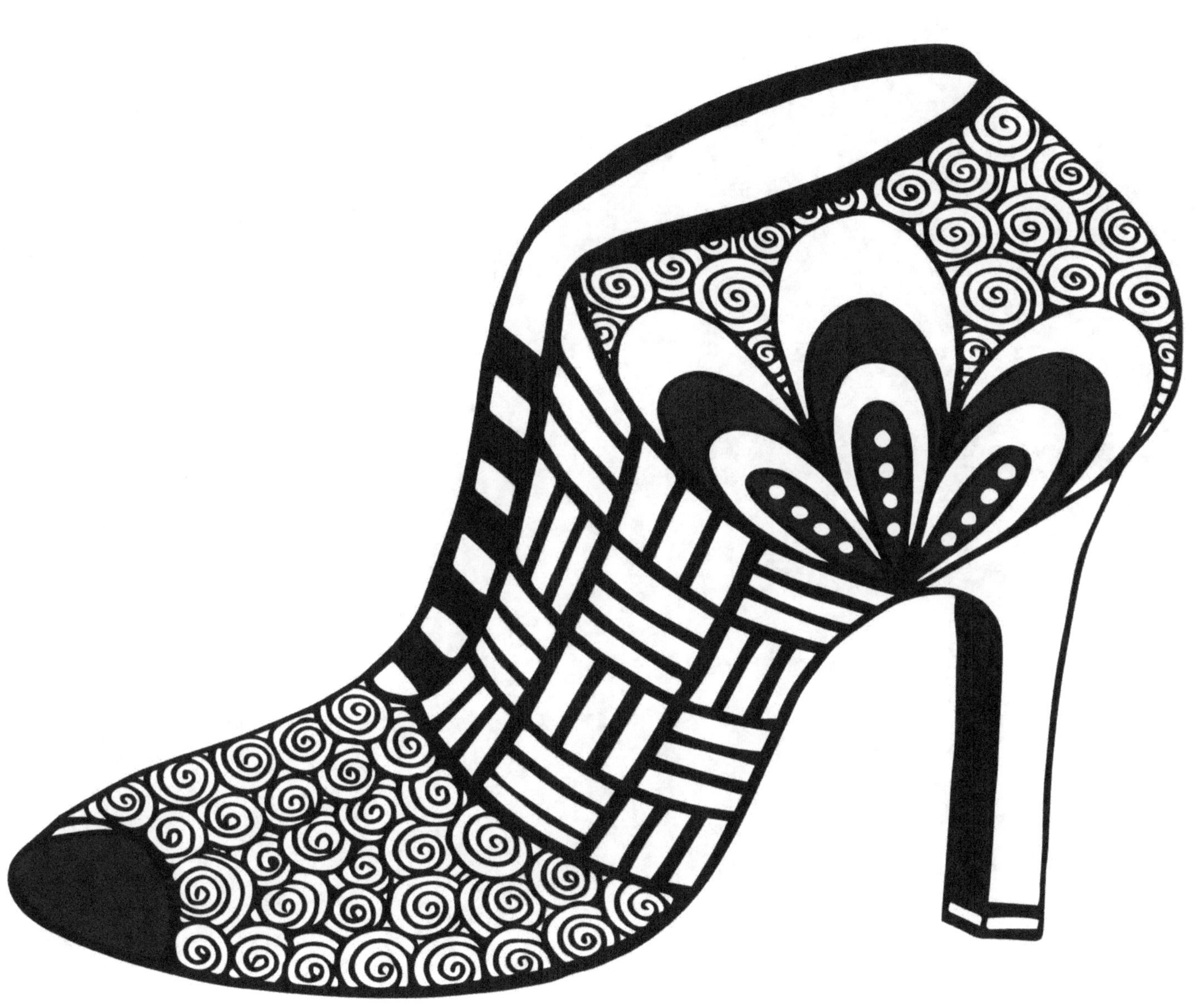

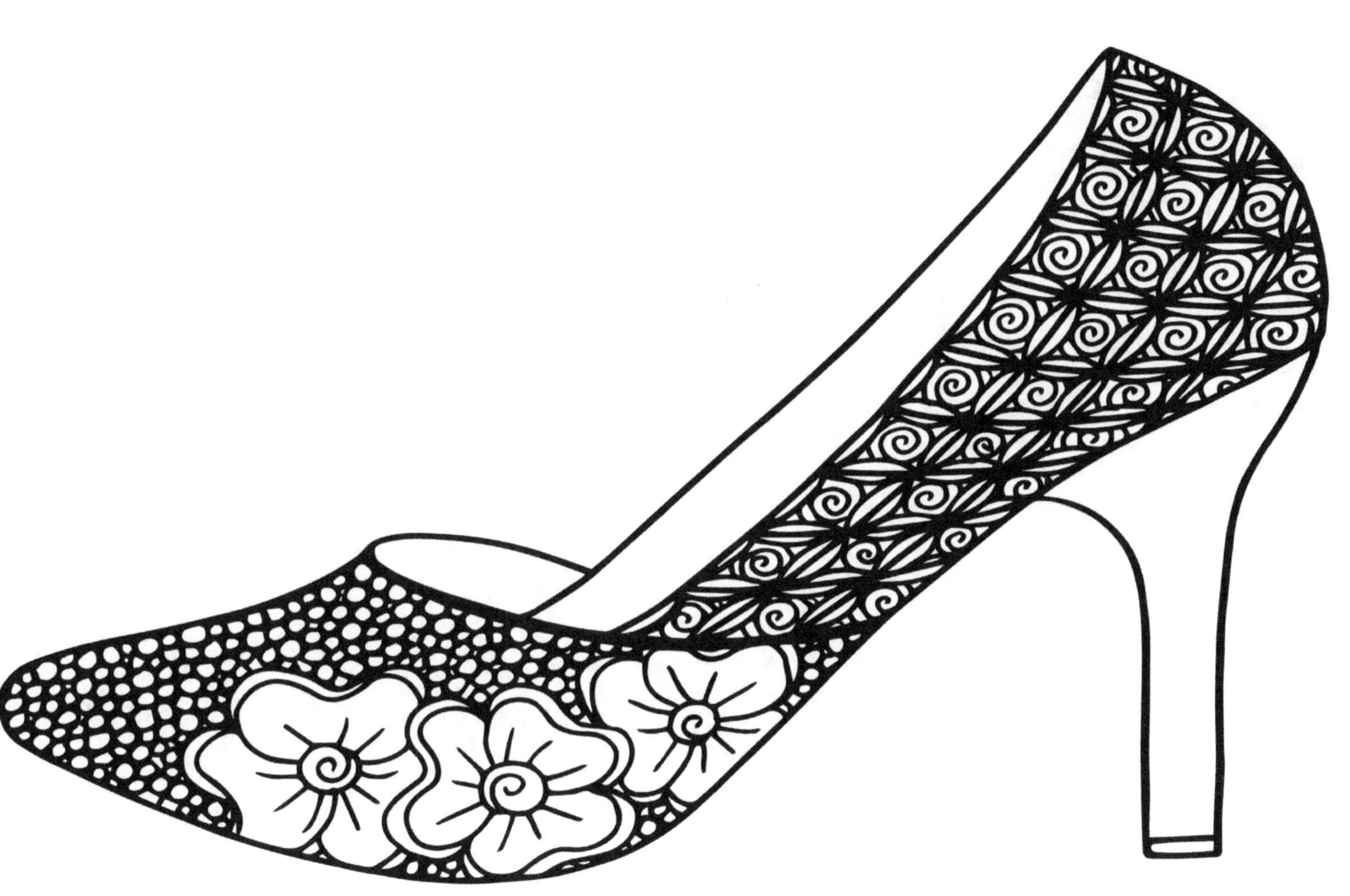

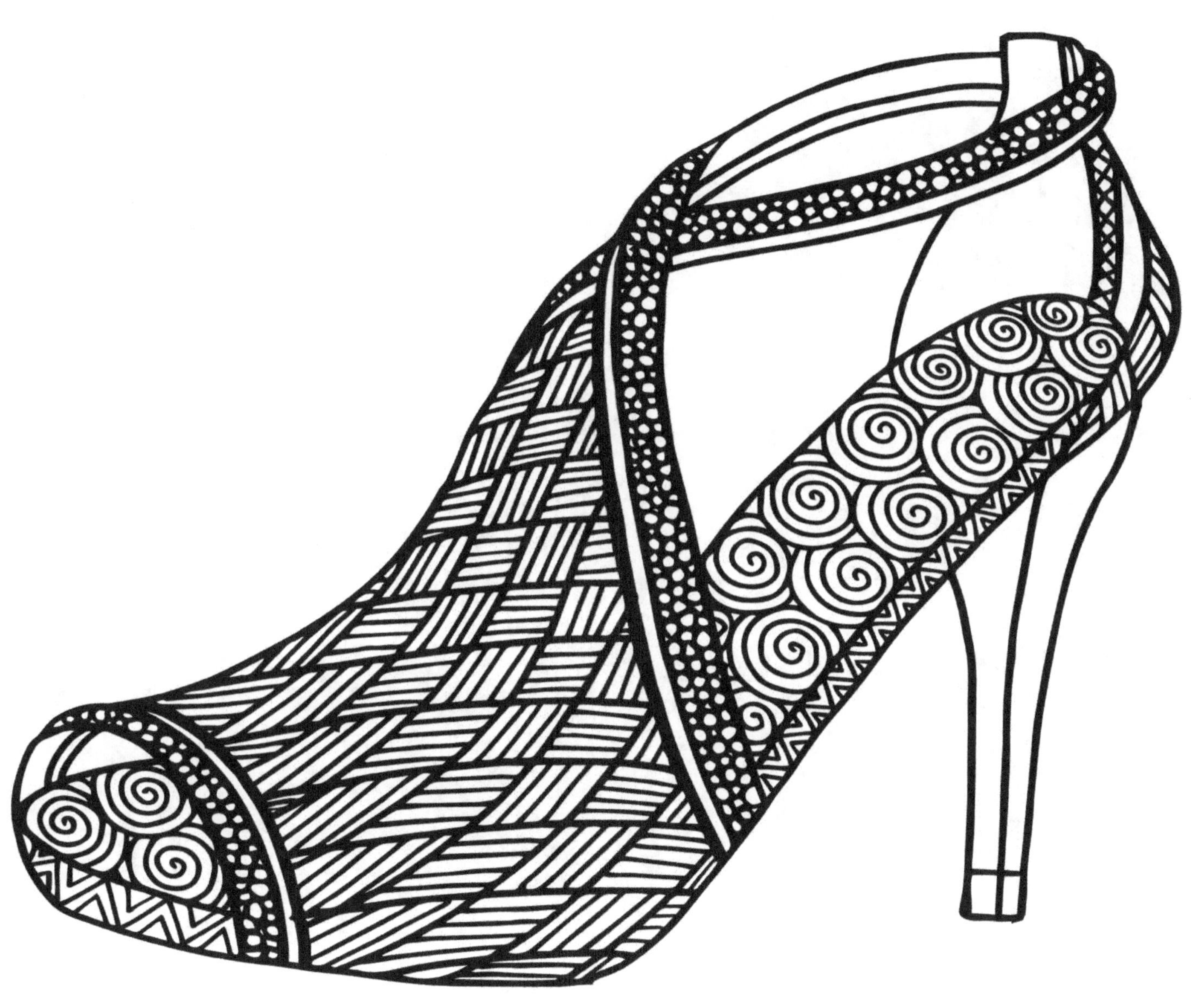

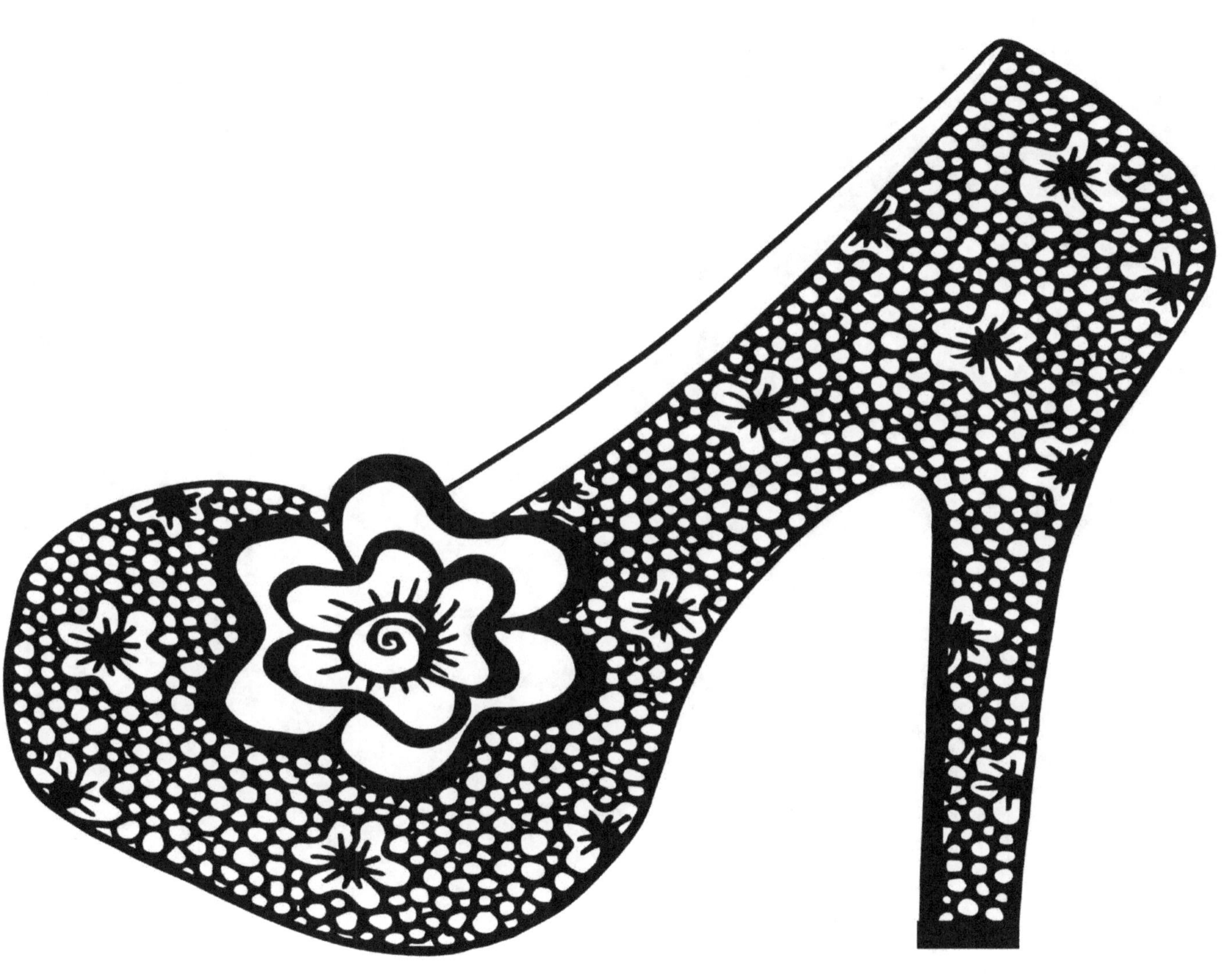

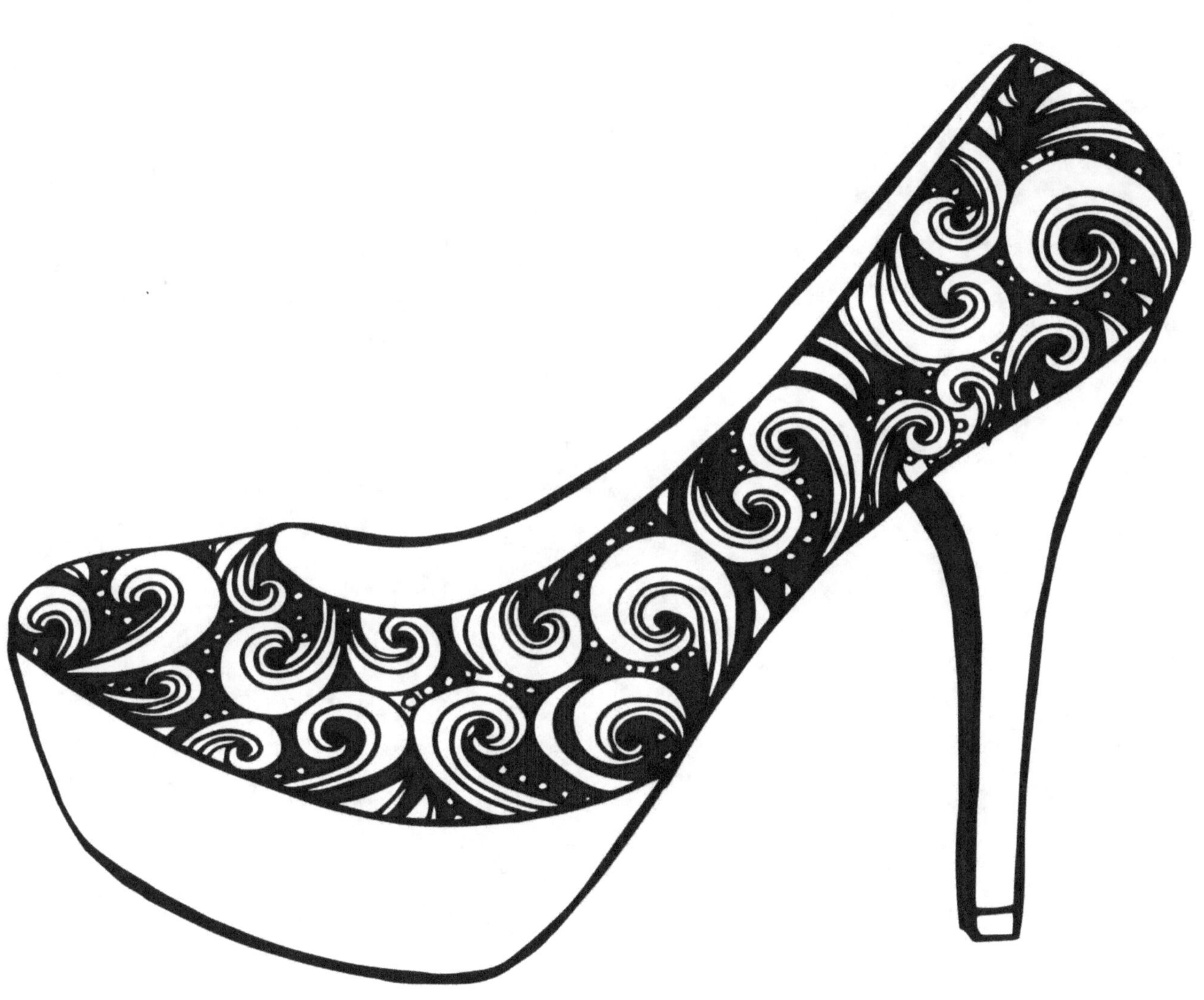

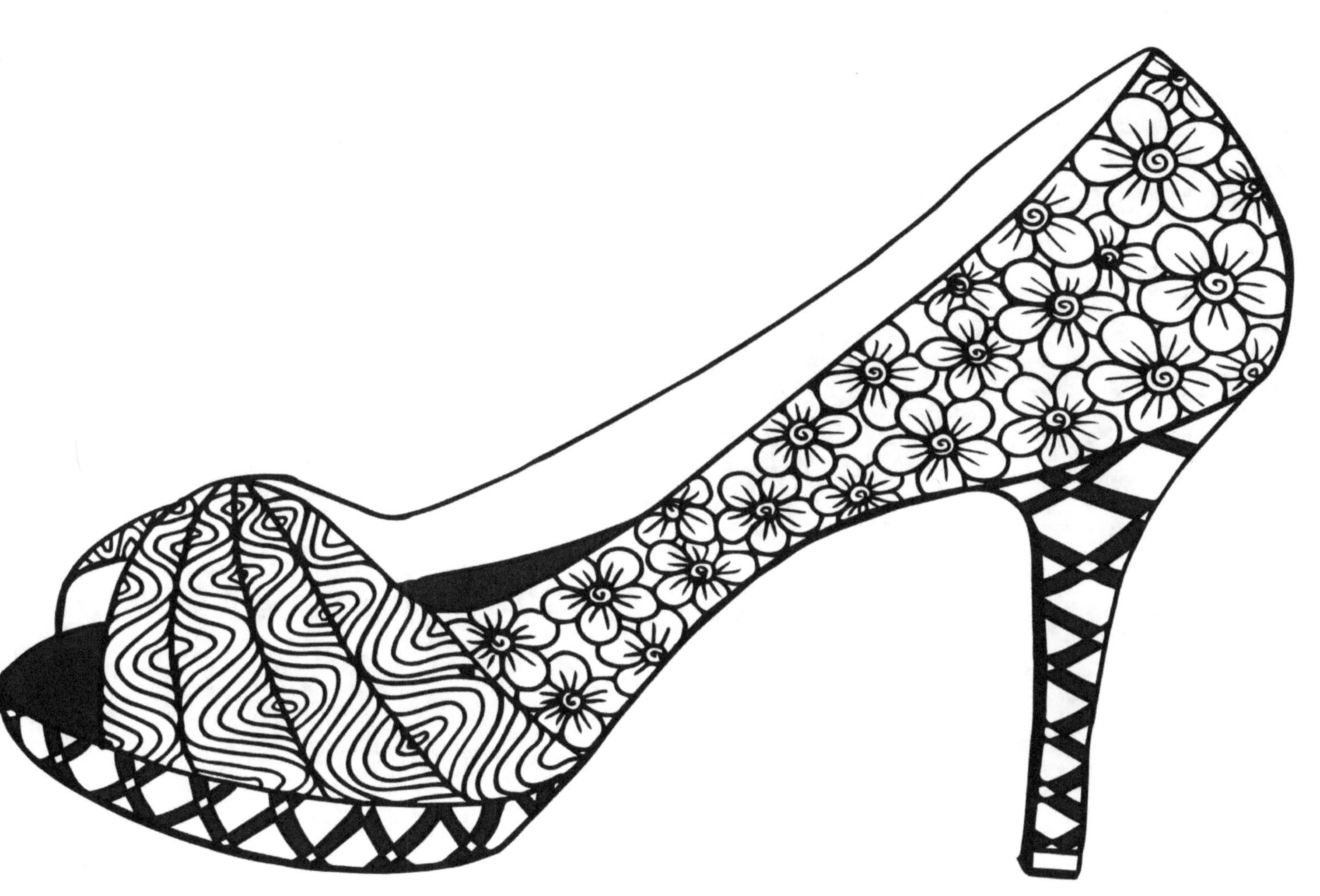

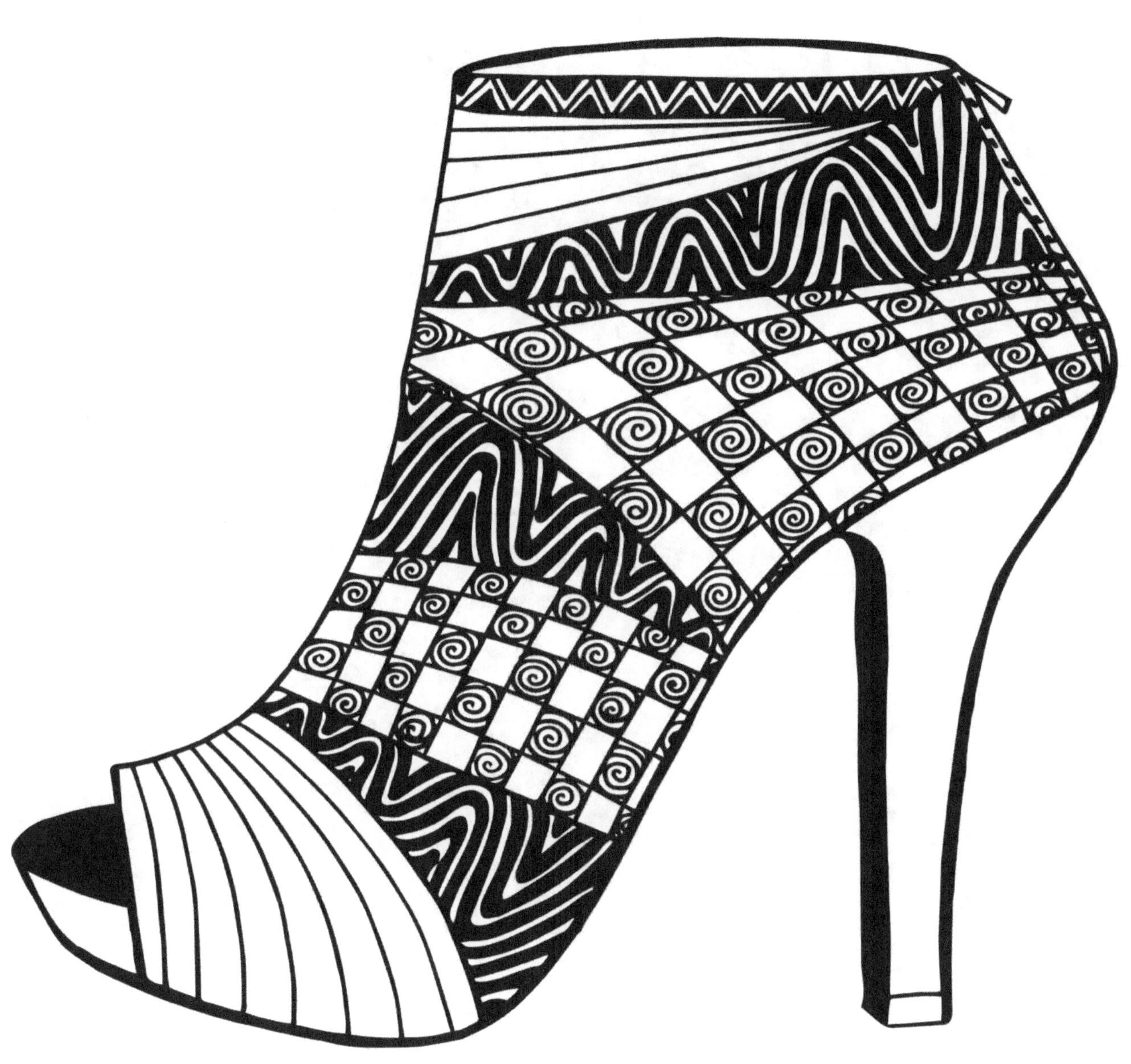

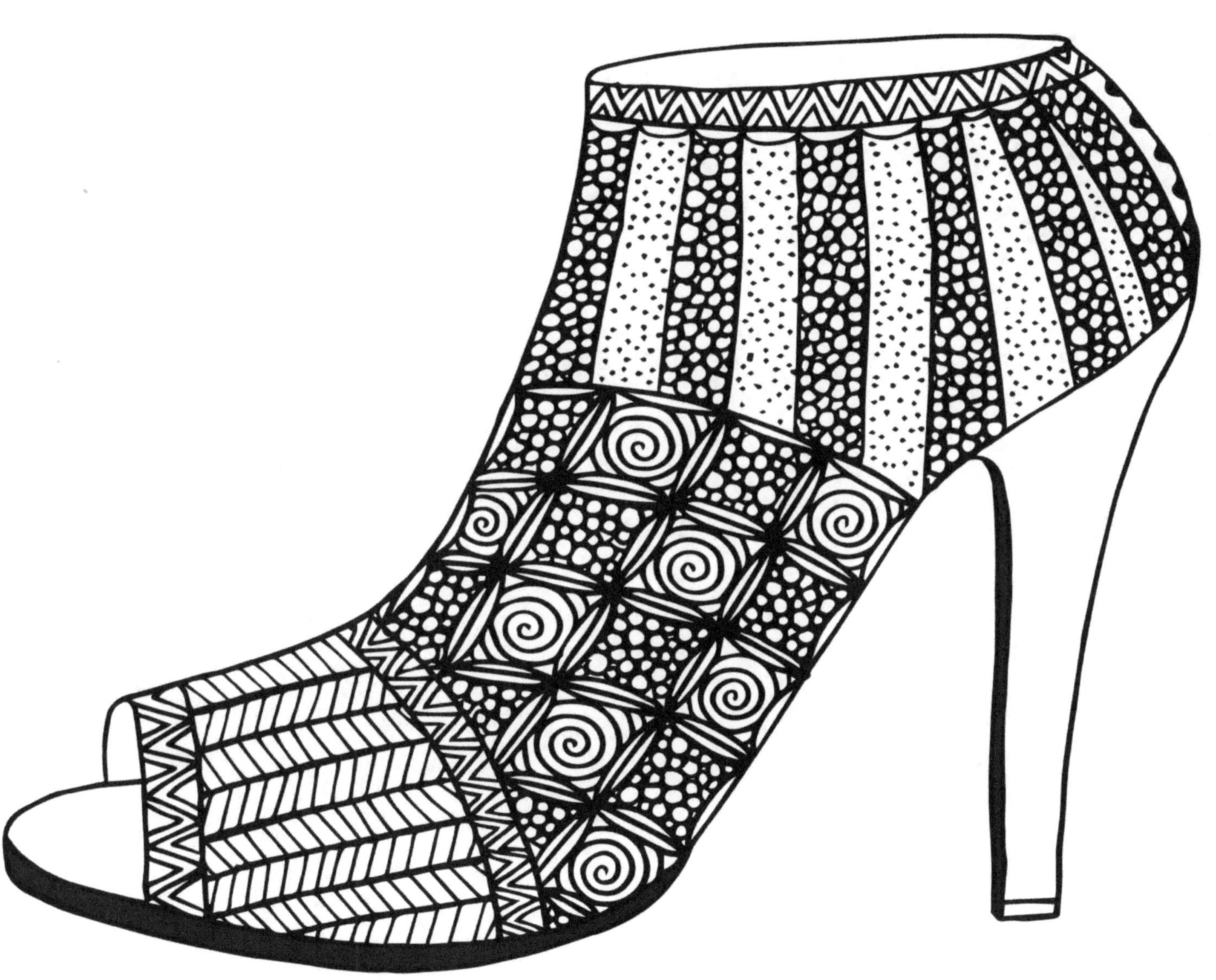

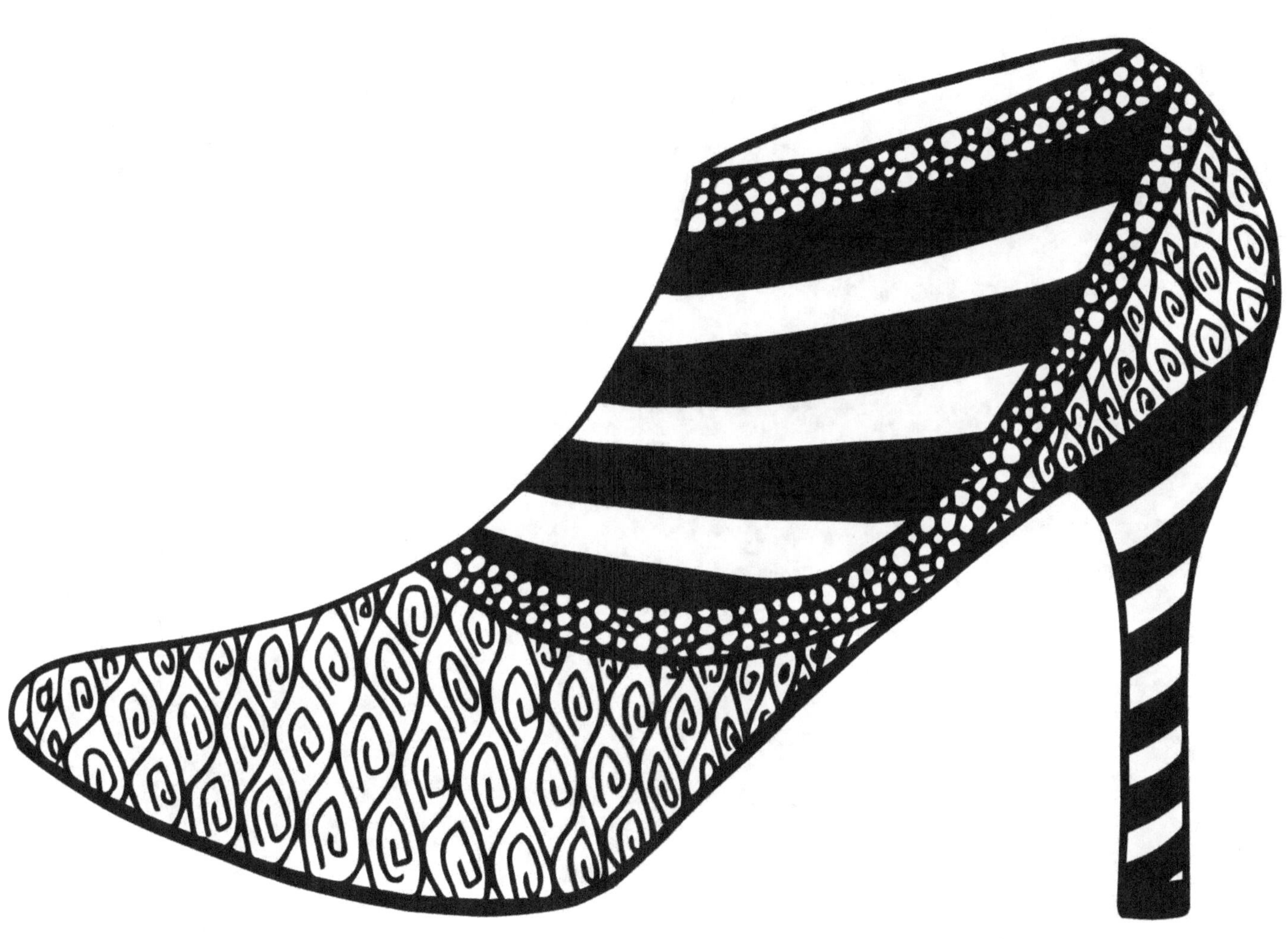

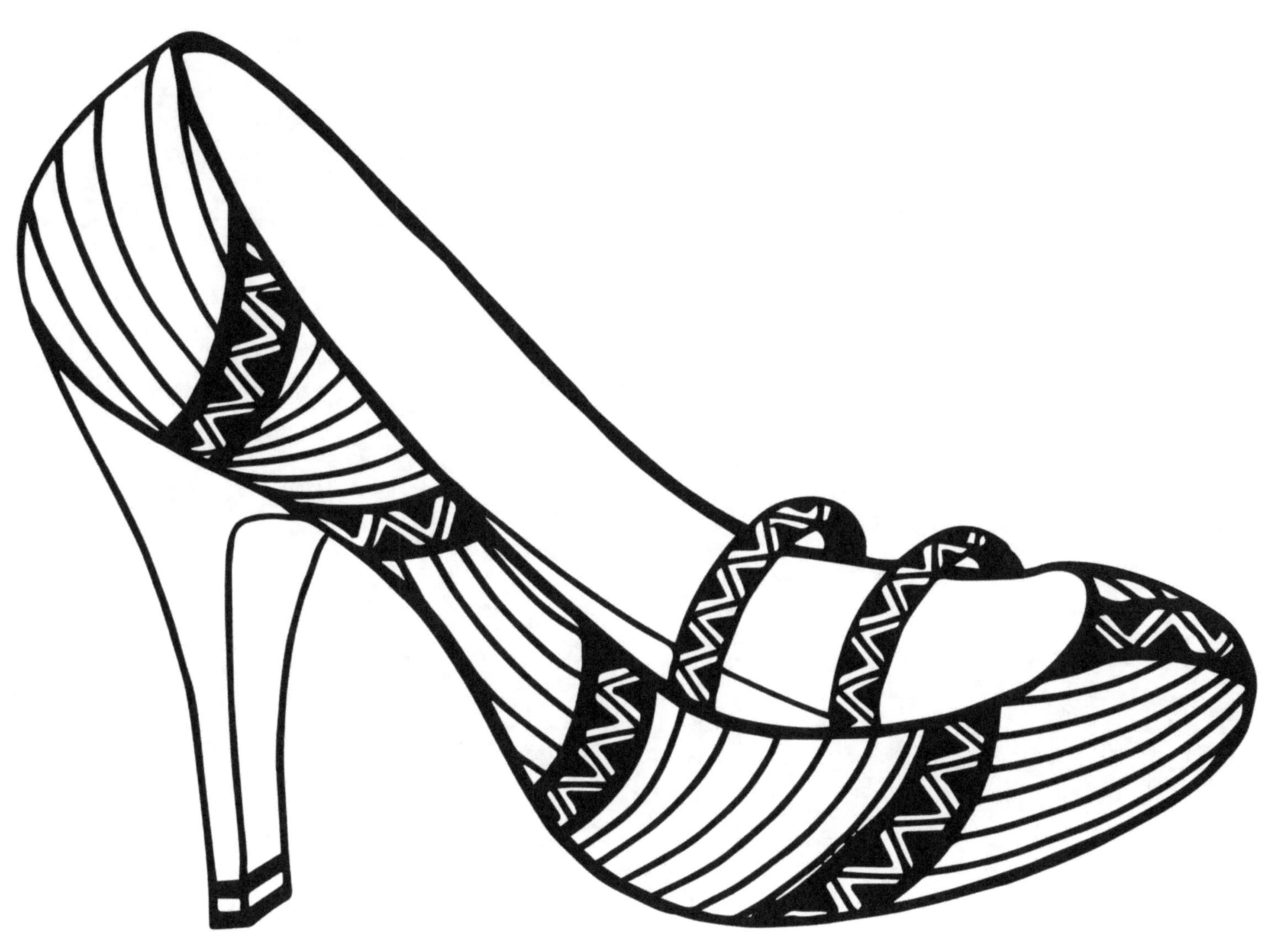

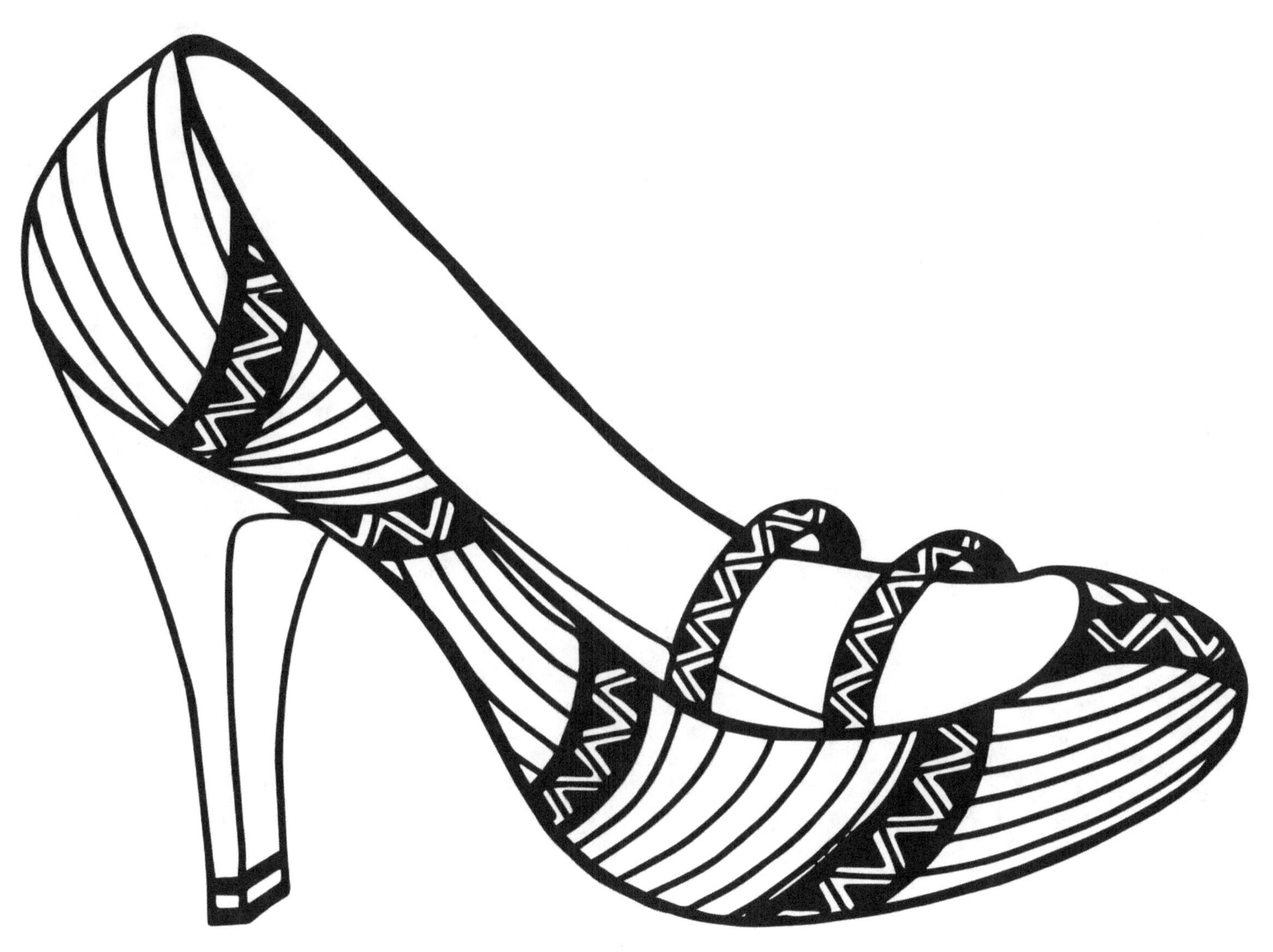